2—

Best Wishes

PROFESSIONAL
DESTINY®
DISCOVER THE CAREER
YOU WERE BORN FOR

VALERIE HAUSLADEN

Professional Destiny is a registered trademark of Valerie Hausladen, Edge Communication Group.

ISBN 978-1442168848

Manufactured in the United States of America.

July 2009

www.professionaldestiny.com

The chain of destiny
can only be grasped one link at a time.

—Sir Winston Churchill

PROFESSIONAL DESTINY

ACKNOWLEDGEMENTS

This book has been a labor of love, and I would like to express my sincere gratitude to all of those who have helped me bring it to life:

To my friend and professional colleague Ken Segall, for designing the book from cover to cover and tirelessly providing edits (I swear he knows every semicolon in this book!). And to *Michael Rylander* for lending his creative genius and adding the perfect touches to the final cover design.

To my faithful early readers Caroline Boudreaux, Trevor Romain, Kelley Burrus, Roberta Gutermuth, Kent Bloomstrand, Stephanie Hausladen and Gregory Durham, for their heartfelt enthusiasm, suggestions and encouragement.

To Leslie Stephen, who read my entire manuscript and provided me with the encouragement to continue—having never met me and asking nothing in return. I consider her an angel.

To Katie Laine, my first life coach, for showing up when I needed her and providing me with inspiration. And to *Karen James* for having the faith to become my first client when I changed careers.

To my mother Virginia Nevitt, for her love and instilling in me during my critical formative years, the belief that I can do anything.

To my sister Sharon Real and her family, Jon, Jonathan and Jacqueline, for their amazing generosity and use of their Telluride home as my writing sanctuary.

To my brother Eric Daly and his wife Bobbi, for their warmth, hospitality and continuous sense of humor… not to mention the gift of my "lucky reindeer."

To my cherished friend Shari Wynne, for her wisdom, encouragement, and infinite love and support.

To Bob Gutermuth, my first friend in Austin, for sharing in endless adventures, being there every step of the way, surprising me with a gift that ignited my enthusiasm for publishing, and most importantly for becoming part of my family.

And to my beautiful, amazing daughters, Stephanie and Allie, for showing me a dimension of love that I never thought possible.

INTRODUCTION

We meet thousands of people in our professional lives. The ones who stand out are those who are passionately involved in their work—and spiritually rewarded. That's because they're doing what they were born to do; they've found a career that allows them to use their natural gift. I call this Professional Destiny, and every one of us has one—whether or not we ever discover it.

This is a book about purpose—a purpose that is spiritual in the sense that it gives our lives richer meaning and deeper satisfaction. This is spirituality as a broad essence, not tied to a particular religious practice or denominational belief.

There is an undertone in this book that reflects a belief that "things happen." Call it synchronicity, chance or coincidence—life's journey is filled with opportunities, setbacks, sheer luck and unpredictable experiences. Whether you believe these things are defined by God, Buddha, Allah, Krishna or any other power or deity, I'm referring to a creative force larger than ourselves. I refer to this force as "the Universe." It's a force that is uniquely perceived by each of us in accordance with our own morals, beliefs and/or religion. To emphasize our individuality, I have chosen to break the rules of consistency and sometimes capitalize the "u" in universe, and sometimes not. Read it as you believe.

Our responsibility is to remember who we are, practice it with full conviction and leave the best legacy we can during our time on earth.

This search for our purpose, our mission, our life's work, is a search for our Professional Destiny.

I

PURPOSE IN LIFE

Oh very young, what will you leave us this time?
You're only dancing on this earth for a short while…

—Cat Stevens

An aspiring engineer feels ambivalent about his work, then finds himself firing up students as a nationally recognized teacher of physics.

A TV account executive feels like something's missing, then finds herself transforming the lives of thousands of needy orphans.

A college dropout follows his inner voice, then finds himself changing the way the world uses computers.

Stories like these are all around us. They're unrelated to economic or educational level. Yet they all have one thing in common: they are stories about people finding themselves.

These are the people who have a passion for what they do, a purpose in life that is clear and undeniable, those who are doing "what they were meant to do." These are the people who are infinitely fulfilled by their day-to-day work.

Have you ever asked yourself why are you here? What exactly are you meant to do? Is there a reason, besides getting through the day, that you're living and breathing on this planet?

It's a big question. Sometimes so big that we quickly skip over it and rationalize that we're not really meant to know. After all, most people don't.

We came here to fulfill a purpose, to reach our highest potential. It is our destiny.

All of us have a purpose. It calls on us to put to use the gifts and talents we were born with. They are custom-designed for each of us and as unique as our fingerprints. We are given these special gifts to apply in our life, and are happiest when they are fully expressed and shared.

Some of us know what our purpose is. Others are beginning the search. Others feel lost and in the dark.

How exactly do we find our purpose? Does it tie in with our profession, or is it separate? The answer is, our lives are integrated. All aspects of our existence are meant to be cohesive and inter-mingled—our professional careers, our personal lives and our spiritual awareness. Since our profession takes up the majority of our day (50%-80% of our waking hours) and our purpose is our lifetime guiding force, it is ultimately both energizing and fulfilling when the two are intertwined.

Finding your purpose and practicing it with your profession is an immensely gratifying and productive experience. You begin to engage in work that you are uniquely suited to do and make a positive impact. You become impassioned, focused and creative. You seek to find meaning and contribute in bigger ways.

When this happens, you've begun the journey to discovering your Professional Destiny—and living it.

Here is a list of indicators that will help you recognize when you are on the right path:

You are engaged. When you're doing what you love, you become passionate about your work and lose track of time. You feel alive, energetic and creative. There is simply not enough time in the day to do what you can't wait to do.

You feel on track. Things come naturally. Work seems easy, though it may not for others—because you're exercising your gift. Your level of satisfaction is your true guidance system.

You feel honest. You're being yourself. You're pursuing a path that is in line with your values and interests, and you're living in true authenticity with yourself.

You become lighter. Being true to your values allows you to shed a huge burden—the burden of maintaining a facade. You instantly experience a sense of relief as the weight is lifted.

You are committed. You clearly set your vision and do what you say you will. You may not know how you are going to get there or when, but you know that you will.

You operate with compassion. Your sense of individual freedom gives you a new sense of community. Your interactions become genuinely rewarding and you create true connections with others.

You make a contribution. What you are doing is meaningful and, while you may be well compensated, your driving force is contribution above money.

You are fulfilled. When you fully express your gifts, talents and creativity, you feel a deep-seated sense of satisfaction. Being on the path to reaching your full potential just feels great.

You make a difference. Your work positively impacts others in a most meaningful way. You're confident that you're leaving a legacy, and you're gratified by that knowledge.

John O'Donohue writes in his book *Anam Cara* that "you were sent to a shape of destiny in which you would be able to express the special gift you bring to the world… there is a unique destiny for each person. Each one of us has something to do here that can be done by no one else… It is in the depths of your life that you will discover the invisible necessity that brought you here. When you begin to discover this, your gift and giftedness come alive. Your heart quickens and the urgency of living re-kindles your creativity."

Each of us is here to discover our purpose and express our giftedness. It is our direction in life. We must find the seed that lies within us and nurture its growth.

When you stop asking "how do I get ahead?" and instead ask "how can I contribute in a meaningful way?" or "what makes me feel whole and complete?" you will be able to combine your unique talent with service to others. This is when you will feel that you have genuinely made a difference; you have truly contributed; your life has meaning. You will notice how it energizes you. The satisfaction is worth its weight in gold. You will reach true fulfill-ment because you are doing what you came here to do.

Ultimately, finding your purpose in life and practicing it every day in your profession is doing your life's work. It is realizing your Professional Destiny.

HOW AND WHEN DO WE FIND OUR PROFESSIONAL DESTINY?

*If you don't know what to do at first,
open your eyes and look for the possibilities.*

—Jacqueline Real (my niece, at age nine)

What is the difference between a job and our life's work?

A job is something we do to earn a living. Oftentimes it is too small for our spirit.

Our life's work is a mighty undertaking that challenges us, taps into our creative energy and reawakens our spirit. It is our work with a capital W. Once we start on the path, the urgency of this work is bigger than us. Our passion and creativity are ignited.

Some people know at a young age what they love to do. Unfortunately they often bury their desire due to conflicting outside influences or a bad experience early on—such as being rejected, humiliated for being different, or having a passion outside of the norm.

Those who recognize their calling early in life and build on it are the lucky ones. Those who gain enough strength or independence to seek a more satisfying path in later life are also lucky. And though they may not feel so fortunate at the time, those compelled to seek change due to sheer discomfort are lucky as well— because despite their own hesitation, events have pushed them in the direction of their true purpose.

Those who are not lucky are the people who ignore their yearnings and go through life in quiet desperation, unfulfilled and suffering from an existence that feels hollow, limited, empty and meaningless.

Anyone can make a change at any time, whenever they feel strong enough. It may be when they reach a financial level that provides a sense of stability, allowing them to feel free. Or when they've reached an emotional point when they've had enough time to know who they are, and have enough distance from early influences (parents, teachers, religion) that may have sidetracked them. It might also be when they feel they have met their primary responsibilities after raising children and fulfilling other obligations. Some people reach a point of frustration in which continuing along the same path becomes unbearable, and they finally decide to do something different.

Essentially you either live long enough to have gathered enough strength, or you have suffered badly enough to finally feel ready to take the risk.

For those of us who don't have that clarity at a young age, a period of disenchantment can be a great blessing.

I reached this pivotal turning point during my mid-thirties. I remember a distinct moment when I was sitting on the porch at my house in Boulder, Colorado, looking across the street at the stunning Flatiron mountains thinking, "to everyone else I look like I have it all: two beautiful daughters, a good husband, friends, a great career, high income, a wonderful house and excellent health— yet deep down I am completely miserable."

Something was missing inside.

It was at that time that I began to yearn to move from a life of success to a life of significance.

I continued in my corporate career for several more years after that, but this poignant moment began my journey of seeking other answers. I started reading voraciously and going to seminars. I tried different churches. I sought out mentors and people I admired who were living lives of meaning. I started participating in opportunities that re-awakened my soul such as volunteering with various organizations and taking eye-opening trips. Some I liked and some I didn't. It was the beginning of a wonderful, challenging and fulfilling journey.

A MOMENT OF TRUTH—ASKING THE QUESTION

The first step is to start asking questions. Questions like:

Why, when things are outwardly going well, do I not feel good inside?

Why am I here? What am I meant to do?

What am I good at?

What interests me and how can I apply these interests to all aspects of my life?

How can I use my gifts to benefit others—at home, in the workplace or in any small way?

Have I been living my own life or a life that someone else wants me to live?

How can I make a contribution I feel good about?

Many people don't want to ask these questions. It's scary. What will they find out? What if it means a significant change? They don't feel prepared. They don't believe they can handle the truth, so they'd rather not know. At this point, change seems too hard so they make a choice to survive in their current situation, rather than thrive in a new one.

Why? We know that the moment we truly admit to something is the moment our life begins to change. Like admitting that our current life situation or profession just doesn't mean anything or fulfill us anymore. Too many of us just don't want to deal with this possibility so we don't even go there. If we do, we don't commit to make a change or take any action, we just talk about it. It seems so much safer. It's like we say to ourselves, I really don't want to see my life that clearly... but by the way, "why am I here?" We are in conflict—consciously or subconsciously—and need to notice and pay attention to it. We want the answer, but on our own terms. Although it seems far more comfortable to choose complacency, the cost is high.

But for those who do sincerely ask the question and want to genuinely know the answer, the journey begins...

2

A VISION SETS THINGS IN MOTION

If you can dream it, you can do it.

—Walt Disney

A ll greatness starts with a vision. You have to see your end game in order to get there. A strong vision is the building block for everything, and without it we can't possibly achieve mastery in our talent or profession.

Have you ever heard of an Olympian who didn't first dream of going to the Olympics?

Here's why we need a vision:

Having a strong vision inspires and guides us to where we want to be, and helps us make decisions. If you clearly set a vision, you won't be distracted and you won't wander aimlessly. If you get off track temporarily, it will be easier to remember your vision and get back on your path.

A clear vision and sense of purpose motivates you. There is no other way to generate the tireless source of energy that you'll need to accomplish your task. And you *will* need a tireless source— because embarking on your journey is a challenging task. It is a perilous journey where you encounter a series of tests, trials and setbacks. Difficulties and barriers are guaranteed to pop up along the way. There is no free lunch when you are pursuing your dream. And the bigger your dream, the bigger the challenges you can expect. However, if your vision is strong enough, you will view barriers as something to cross over, not as something that blocks your way. You see the end state and you have the motivation to pick yourself up after a setback in order to get there.

While watching the winter Olympics several years ago, I was struck by Sasha Cohen's focused determination in women's figure skating. Going into the competition she was the favorite. However, during the final four-minute free program she had a skating disaster in the first twenty seconds of her program, falling on her first jump and stepping out of her next triple-flip attempt. It looked like she was completely out of contention and that she would have no medal at all. Instead she rebounded, skating flawlessly to finish her program with strength and class, delivering a truly unbelievable performance. As each contender followed, everyone watched to see if Sasha could overcome the odds and win a medal. It seemed impossible at first, but she did. Her comeback was brilliant and enough to win a silver medal. Asked in an interview what went through her mind when she was skating after such a disappointing start, she said, "I just told myself to stay determined and keep believing."

You can't do this without a vision.

What makes a vision strong? A great vision is a clear statement of your purpose. It is:

Memorable

Concise

Aspirational

Simple

Easily repeatable

Relevant

Something you honestly believe

A strong vision is something you can remember in a moment's notice; it is an image you can call up on demand. It is a declaration of what you want to accomplish. It represents your deepest, most authentic goals and interests.

Most of all, a great vision is a vivid description of your desired end state. It creates a picture in your mind of the future you want.

You must "see" yourself achieving your vision. You must see yourself winning a medal at the Olympics, you must see yourself as the successful leader of a company, you must see yourself as a world famous musician delighting a crowd.

Here are examples of two famous visions that changed the course of history:

John F. Kennedy said in 1960: "By the end of the decade, we will put a man on the moon and bring him home safely." To achieve that goal, NASA had to overcome seemingly insurmountable obstacles. It did.

Martin Luther King said in 1963: "I have a dream... that one day this nation will rise up and live out the true meaning of its creed: 'We hold these truths to be self-evident, that all men are created equal'...." This simple, powerfully-worded vision for the future defined the course of equality and served to inspire people for decades.

And what follows are some visions of everyday heroes whose stories are featured in this book:

"I will be a teacher and haunt my students with a passion for Physics."

"I will become a published author and write books that help children cope with their illnesses, fears, stress and grief."

"I will transform the lives of India's orphans by fulfilling their basic rights to love, nourishment, shelter and education."

ORGANIZATIONAL VISION

It is also important for companies to have a clear vision. A strong vision sets a solid company foundation and gives employees a shared purpose to rally behind.

Bill Gates started Microsoft and his early vision for the company was:

"A computer on every desk and in every home."

In the 1970s and early 1980s, when the first computers were just being introduced, this vision seemed like nothing more than a fantasy. Back then, people were still using expensive mainframes and the software came from the same company that built the computer. In 1975, when Microsoft was founded, Gates dreamed that computers would be "ubiquitous and indispensable" and "massive computer networks would put the world's knowledge at our fingertips." Now, every year, computers are becoming smaller, faster and cheaper, and the internet provides everyone with a powerful, global network. It all started with a vision.

Visions can change. In 2000, Gates' purpose expanded beyond the corporate world to philanthropy. He and his wife started the Bill and Melinda Gates Foundation and six years later, the Gates Foundation endowment totaled $33 billion. Bill Gates also announced he would transition from his CEO position at Microsoft Corporation to work full-time for the foundation, beginning in 2008.

Bill Gates expanded his remarkable visionary and management skills to benefit an entirely new cause. The two guiding principles for the Gates Foundation are:

All lives—no matter where they are being led—have equal value.

To whom much has been given, much is expected.

These guiding principles provide the vision for the organization, set the values and identify the expectations for how people should act. And the vision has caught on outside of the foundation. U.S. investor Warren Buffett pledged to give 10 million shares of Berkshire Hathaway stock worth $31 billion at the time of donation to the foundation to further its philanthropic mission. He told the Gates Foundation: "You are tackling problems that have resisted great intellect and lots of money. These are important problems. It's a great feeling to know that as the company (Berkshire Hathaway) becomes worth more and more money, it actually translates into something good around the world." The compelling vision of the foundation, as well as the commitment behind it (both personal and financial), create a powerful force for inspiring good will and generosity.

A strong vision is essential for both individuals and organizations. In both cases it relies heavily on intuition and dreams. For individuals and leaders of organizations, it may come at a quiet moment as a sudden flash of inspiration. It might come to you during a hot shower. Or while you are on a long, peaceful walk through the woods, driving in your car or laying on a beach.

An organizational vision, because it is shared, must inspire others. Therefore it can be more challenging to set. So how do you come up with a strong shared vision?

One way is to brainstorm with a small group. Talk about key words and phrases related to the vision that resonate with each person, and spur each other into dreaming about things that are worth working hard for. The shared vision should solidify the group toward common goals, values and understanding of purpose. Once you have brainstormed the key words and phrases, ask one or two people (hint: don't try to do this with group consensus and save yourself painful rounds of hashing back and forth) to draft a statement based on the shared ideas. Then have them bring it back to the initial group and tweak until you have something that people can share and rally around... with enthusiasm!

SETTING YOUR GOAL—THINK BIG!

The secret of life is to have a task, something
you devote your entire life to… and the most
important thing is—it must be something you
cannot possibly do.

—Henry Moore

A good vision should be larger than your current abilities.

A small vision can limit your success, so make it bigger than what you currently know how to do. If you know exactly how to get to your goal, you're not setting your sights high enough. Expand your sights!

When your vision is big, expect that there will be a gap between where you currently are and where you want to be. It may not be comfortable, but if you think about it, this makes perfect sense. How can there not be a gap? Our task is to get comfortable in the gap, stay focused and keep taking one step at a time. All you need to do is take the first step and the next one will appear. At some point you'll look up and realize that the gap is smaller than when you started out. This will encourage and motivate you.

Release yourself from limiting beliefs that keep you stuck. Take a stand for your self-worth and for who you are, based on your vision. Keep declaring it to yourself and believe in it. Begin to share your vision with the people in your life. Talking about it will help it become more real for you.

Although it may not feel like it, each one of us is well equipped to start our journey.

When you are on course, you will have help as you need it. Look for mentors and those whose experience can guide you. Create relationships. Sometimes, someone will show up unexpectedly at just the right moment in your journey to give you the information you're seeking. If you are in alignment with your path, you will have all the resources that you need. You just have to be on the lookout for them.

FIND YOUR INTEREST AND DO WHAT YOU LOVE

The master in the art of living makes little distinction
between his work and his play, his labor and his leisure,
his mind and his body… he hardly knows which is which.
He simply pursues his vision of excellence in whatever
he does, leaving others to decide whether he is
working or playing. To him he's always doing both.

—James Michener

How do you begin to find your gift? You may have had an awareness of it as a child. Maybe as a yearning you felt in your heart, but perhaps that yearning got buried under a suffocating blanket of responsibility, such as:

- What our parents want us to do (parental aspirations).

- What is most accepted in society (social expectations).

- The need to survive (financial pressures).

- An educational upbringing geared toward spreading your baseline of knowledge across many subjects, not an intentional and personalized search for your greatest potential (institutionalization).

Your gift can be "spiky." Meaning that you are incredibly good at one, two or three things as opposed to being well-rounded in many things. These few things are where to focus. Weaknesses should be acknowledged and developed just enough so that they don't hold you back or get in the way of your progress. But beyond that, there is a diminishing rate of return on the effort spent in trying to strengthen them. You need to be conscious, responsible and ensure that your weaknesses do not harm you, your vision or others. Beyond that, find the areas you excel at and focus your effort in building your skills and experience there.

In June of 2005, Steve Jobs, CEO and cofounder of Apple Computer and then-CEO of Pixar Animation Studios, delivered the commencement speech at Stanford University. He urged the graduates to pursue their dreams and do what they love, and to see the opportunities in life's setbacks. He reflected on his very public, humiliating ousting from Apple in 1985 and said, "I didn't see it then, but it turned out that getting fired from Apple was the best thing that could have ever happened to me. It freed me to enter one of the most creative periods of my life."

During the next five years, Jobs went on to found Pixar Studios and NeXT Computer. Pixar soon created the hugely successful animated feature film, *Toy Story,* and became one of the most acclaimed animation studios in the world. Then, in a synchronous turn of events, Apple bought NeXT and Jobs returned to Apple, where he soon became CEO.

Jobs told the students, "I'm pretty sure none of this would have happened if I hadn't been fired from Apple. It was awful-tasting medicine, but I guess the patient needed it. Sometimes life hits you in the head with a brick. Don't lose faith. I'm convinced that the only thing that kept me going was that I loved what I did. You've got to find what you love… and the only way to do great work is to love what you do. If you haven't found it yet, keep looking. Don't settle. As with all matters of the heart, you'll know when you find it. And, like any great relationship, it just gets better and better as the years roll on. So keep looking until you find it. Don't settle."

The following story is about a young man who followed his heart and didn't settle. He made a decision, released limiting expectations of what he "should do" and followed his passion to become a teacher. Since that decisive moment, he experienced the momentum of things building and getting better and better as time goes on. He loves what he does and his department has now been acclaimed as one of the best in the world.

LIGHTING UP A CLASSROOM—A TEACHER'S STORY

On December 17th, 2004, Westlake High School in Austin, TX was identified by the College Board as having the strongest AP Physics course in the United States. Among other high schools its size, Westlake had the highest proportion of students receiving scores of three or higher (on a scale of five). It also had the highest-performing AP physics students among all schools worldwide. Here is the story of one of Westlake's master teachers, Mark Misage.

"A lot of my family is in education, including my favorite aunt and uncle. As a youngster, I was fascinated by all things mechanical. I was always tinkering, ripping cars apart, so I knew I was going to do something mechanical. My dad is an engineer, though, and by the time I went to college, I thought that I wanted to go into engineering. The dollar signs were definitely calling me that way. It took about a semester in college, however, to realize that money is not the end-all, be-all. I just wasn't having a whole lot of fun. I had always thought that I would love to teach. In my college psychology class, I gave a presentation and I had so much fun and had such an adrenaline rush when I stood up in front of the class, I knew that this was something I was meant to do. For a while I continued on the engineering path but I was bored and grumpy. Finally I made the decision to teach and it was like a big burden was lifted.

I knew that my parents weren't going to be super happy that I was getting out of engineering. But as soon as I told them, after a semester in my freshman year, everything changed.

Looking back I can see that teaching was something I always wanted to do and if it would pay more, it would have been a no-brainer. But the discontent I felt before I made the decision to leave engineering was a good thing. It got me to move. And from that point on, I have considered myself to be an incredibly lucky person.

Once I made that decision, everything just sort of fell in line. From the beginning it clicked. I didn't really pursue this job. I grew up in Austin, so I thought "well don't even try to apply at Westlake" since it was considered to be the top public high school in the city. One of my professors told me there was an opening and told me to get my application in tomorrow. I figured I didn't have anything to lose so I put in an application, but I didn't get the job. I was told I was too young. It was kind of a hoot because on the day of the interview, I felt like I looked really young. I normally wear contacts but I wore glasses and it was in the summertime and unbelievably hot outside and I didn't have air conditioning in my car. When I went to the interview in an air-conditioned building, my glasses fogged up. It was horrible. I didn't get that one. The woman who did get it, though, taught up until spring break and then resigned, so immediately they called me and asked if I would take it. They didn't even finish the sentence before I said yes.

I started at Westlake High School in 1989. The place was so different. There was one physics teacher and maybe a couple of classes, but I was lucky... I met Dan Harper. He was teaching physical science and I was teaching physics and I learned so many amazing tricks from him. He's really innovative and I grabbed on to his coattails. We wrote a curriculum together. When we were both teaching physics the numbers of students signing up for the class started exploding. There are six physics teachers now.

I met my wife Nancy at Westlake. She did the exact same thing as I did. She started as a graduate in molecular biology but then realized that she's very much a people person and there wasn't a whole lot of interaction going on in the lab. She made the decision to go into teaching and went back to get her teaching certificate while getting her masters in science education. That's when we met. It wouldn't have happened if I hadn't made the decision to teach.

The reason I think that physics is so successful at Westlake is because we go out of our way to make everything we do relevant to the class. No matter what we're presenting that day up at the chalkboard, for that moment it's the coolest thing we've ever seen. We're passionate about it and it's real. If you're just standing up there rattling something off and then you work a problem at the board and you're sort of bored with it, then the students are sort of bored with it and it becomes self-perpetuating. That's the thing with this job, being that into it takes a lot of energy but at the end of the day, I ask myself "Where did the day go?" I need this period to be an hour longer. It's cool that you can shut your door, you're in charge and for 150 people you're deciding how much fun they're going to have and how much they learn.

We really enjoy our job and go out of our way to try to make it rigorous and educational, yet fun. So I don't think we take ourselves too seriously. You get this strange aura around physics classes usually that they're tough. A tough topic, incredibly rigorous. We're not like that. We make a lot of it a game to make it enjoyable.

For example, today we talked about the traffic lights on Highway 360. Have you ever considered that they have to think about how they hang the traffic lights? That's the kind of problems we'll do on the board. Let's say they put a traffic light up on a day like today when it's nice and sunny and warm and they pull the cable nice and tight. Well when the first big Blue Northern comes in and it gets really cold, metals contract so the cable will get shorter. The tension in the cable will skyrocket and it could snap, so they always have to leave a sag to leave room for the contraction. We work the problem on the board. Did you see the traffic light? Everything we do, we point to something they'll see. Every day. We explain stuff you see all the time.

Tomorrow we're breaking out the Barbie Doll and we're going to determine Barbie's center of mass. We're introducing a concept called torque and we put her on balances. We basically weigh her on two balances and figure out where her center of mass is. It's something we could just do up on the board but it's kind of cool to break out the Barbie Doll.

Earlier, we shot a dart gun at a stuffed bear to explain two-dimensional motion. Rather than drawing something on the chalkboard, we shot a bear with a blow-dart gun. We calculated the velocity of the dart coming out of the gun with nothing but a meter stick.

I still get that rush I felt back in my college psychology class when I teach. And my wife is the same way. We're on a high all through the day.

By the end of the year I want the students haunted by physics. I want to completely change their view of the universe. Everything they see… I want them to see through the eyes of physics. That is my goal.

I really think it's fate that I'm teaching. If what you're doing is not fun, you shouldn't do it; you have to be having fun because you put so much time into it. I have as much fulfillment as I would want. I get my charge from the students. For me, it's being up performing in front of the class and it's seeing the light come on in their faces. It's not the pay—that's the challenge. It's seeing the performance of the students and hearing back from them. A few are actually teaching physics now and a lot of them have become physics majors… that just stuns me. And, of course, it's a blast working with my peers.

I'm real happy with what I've done in my life and I've never looked back."

3

THE GREAT CRASH

Yeah, I miss the old crowd sometimes
And the wild, wild nights of running
You know, a starving soul can't live like that for long
You go around in circles that just keep getting smaller
You wake up one morning and half your life is gone

—Don Henley, *Everything is Different Now*

Disenchantment is a motivating force to drive change in your life. No one ever says "hey, things are going really well... I think it's time to change." Most people don't change when they are feeling totally comfortable. They change when they are uncomfortable. Disenchantment is a great motivator. In his story of deciding to become a teacher, Mark Misage said "the discontent I felt before I made the decision to leave engineering was a good thing. It got me to move." He wasn't happy as an engineer—he had chosen the field simply because it paid more. After struggling through engineering for several months, he made a conscious choice to pursue his interests regardless of the financial consequences. His choice took courage—he sacrificed money for fulfillment, but he realized that the true cost to him of not making this sacrifice was even greater. Finally, once he made the choice, a weight was lifted and things seemed to fall into place. He experienced the rush of doing what he loves and making a difference in people's lives every day.

DISENCHANTMENT

When humans find themselves surrounded by nothing but objects,
the response is always one of loneliness.

—Brian Swimme

People who look outside themselves or in material goods for their happiness, isolate themselves and are often not genuinely happy.

Purpose is not being outwardly successful. Purpose is finding your direction. Many people are outwardly successful, but they might not feel that they've done something of value.

You may accumulate a lot in this world, but are you fulfilled?

Abraham Maslow presents his famous *Hierarchy of Needs* as a triangle. At the base are Physical Survival Needs and the Need for Safety and Security. Above those needs are Social Needs such as Belonging and the Need for Self-Esteem. At the top is the Need for Self-Actualization.

Maslow's theory suggests that each individual's needs must be satisfied at the lower levels before they progress to the higher levels. There is no guilt in having abundance—we can help others more when we are liberated. When we have our survival needs met, and are not caught up in the "always wanting more" trap, we are freed up to focus on making a powerful, genuine contribution.

Money is beautiful when used for good. To illustrate this point, Warren Buffet's pledge of $31 billion dollars to the Gates Foundation showed everyone that wealth can be used to make the world a better place. Buffet chose to put the money into service rather than hoard sums so much greater than he would ever need. Following his historic donation, the *Houston Chronicle* wrote:

"His gift is the final lesson in his lifetime of instruction on wealth accumulation: In the end it's not about the money, it's about what you do with it."

Warren Buffet and Bill Gates are two high-profile examples of people who have moved from success to significance.

For the rest of us, having enough financially enables us to be less distracted. If we are constantly struggling to make ends meet, we have less time, money and resources to help others and we might not get the luxury of pursuing our dream right away. We often ignore our yearnings and choose practicality instead. I made this choice when I was choosing my major in college. At 18, I could care less about what I loved doing, I was interested first and foremost in paying my bills. I loved writing and psychology, but saw no successful career in either and chose economics (the closest undergraduate major to business) instead. To me it was a choice of survival vs. fun. Fun was a luxury and I didn't feel secure enough to do what I loved at that point in my life.

Looking back, my interest in writing started in grade school, when I had the first memorable experience in an inconspicuous fourth grade assignment to summarize Chaucer's *Canterbury Tales*. Our class was asked to summarize a full section of one of the *Canterbury Tales* into a two-page document—capturing the essence and primary details while making it concise. We could not exceed two pages. As I worked on my assignment, I got totally engrossed and completely lost track of time. Finally, I turned in my assignment with pride—knowing that I had done my best, and with a deeply satisfied feeling that it was good. My teacher raved about my work and I felt for a moment as if I were on cloud nine. It was the beginning of my interest in writing.

Years later after being far more interested in rebelling as a teenager, and completely forgetting about this experience and writing in general, I had another awakening moment. It happened when fate put me in Mrs. Moser's advanced English class entering my senior year in high school. Mrs. Moser was considered to be a no-nonsense teacher who was extremely tough. Most of my friends thought she was scary, but I—the rebellious teenager—quickly came to love her! Right away she encouraged my talent in writing and persuaded me to enter three essay contests. So I did. I entered three separate essays with three different writing styles, and to my surprise, won each category.

I am convinced that my writing was one major reason why I got accepted to Stanford University. Since I was not the highest-ranking student in my school, I knew I was coming from a disadvantage during the application process, so I enclosed my creative writing essay called "The Mopers" (an amusing tale written about people who slink around feeling sorry for themselves instead of dealing with life's setbacks) along with my application, and somehow managed to squeak in.

By this time I realized that I had a gift and that I loved to write. The problem was that although most of my childhood I had come from a middle class background, my family suffered significant financial hardships during my teenage years. Because of this I qualified for a full financial aid package, yet became 100% focused on survival and getting ahead. At 18, it didn't matter what I loved to do and what I was good at, I couldn't see any way to make a decent living being an English major so I chose Economics. It didn't matter that I didn't like it and that I wasn't particularly great at it. I thought Economics would get me the best job out of school, so that's what I did. Now I clearly see why many have noted that "college is wasted on the youth."

Luckily, the position I took coming out of Stanford was as a pricing analyst in the marketing department of a large corporation, which gave me an entrée into a profession I came to really love. A few years later, I became a marketing copywriter for a huge product launch. It got me noticed and launched my career.

I always wanted to write a book, so I decided it was time to follow my own Professional Destiny and do what I was meant to do.

When I look back, I realize that it took me until my forties to feel brave enough to be able to take the risk to leave the profession I had known for my entire career and become a writer.

Most people living in first-world countries today get to a point where they don't need to worry about their physical survival, safety and security needs. Not at the most basic levels anyway. There is more opportunity to focus on self-actualization or your purpose and what you are "born to do."

Although most of us reach the point where our basic survival needs are met, we often don't notice when we have reached the point of enough and we fall into the trap of "always wanting more." This wanting is insatiable, much to the dismay of our higher calling and true sense of fulfillment.

Many people confide in me that at some point in their careers, they feel as if they've come to a fork in the road. They have reached a level of success and confidence and now they need to make a choice between pursuing an unknown road toward fulfillment, or choosing the familiar path that feels secure. One client so aptly put it, "I know I can go work for company XYZ and make six figures if I want a mind-numbing job, but I don't. Now what do I do?"

It's a challenging choice. On the one hand, if you decide to bite the bullet and pursue a deep yearning that you have, you are often venturing into the unknown—especially if it's very different from the career you've known. You are venturing into unfamiliar territory and you can expect to feel significant anxiety over this. If, on the other hand, you settle and choose not to take that next step forward, you can expect to feel a deep-seated sense of disappointment followed by a sense of lethargy and possibly a low-level or high-level depression. Many people try to mask these feelings by keeping themselves "numbed" through alcohol, prescription drugs or anything that takes their focus away from the fact that they are ignoring a message from their soul. Others simply try to keep frantically busy and convince themselves that they are so important, that they don't have time to notice the uneasiness from within.

Once you are on your path, you can't turn back. A life without purpose will never satisfy you again. It becomes intolerable to sit still and do nothing. You'll reach a point of complete internal friction if you rest on your laurels and do not pursue it.

Lynne Twist, in her book *The Soul of Money,* writes, "People with excess wealth—not all of them, but many—struggle in lives disconnected from the qualities of the soul. They live trapped in the prison of privilege in which material comforts are plentiful, but spiritual and emotional deprivation are real and painful. In that prison, they lose touch with the values of the heart…"

She also discusses that when we become primarily focused on money, "we become smaller. We scramble or race to 'get what's ours.' We often grow selfish, greedy, petty, fearful or controlling, or sometimes confused, conflicted or guilty. We see ourselves as winners or losers, powerful or helpless, and we let those labels deeply define us in ways that are inaccurate... visions of possibility dissolve."

A trap that we are all susceptible to, especially in the Western world, is that we overlook the concept of having enough and become greedy. We come to never fully enjoy what we have because we are always thinking about what we don't yet have (a nicer home or car, more possessions, a bigger company, more money, finer art). This sense of wanting more is an insatiable hunger. It is poison to our soul and kills new, creative possibilities because it locks us into a pattern. It might make our life more comfortable but it doesn't bring us true fulfillment, which only comes when we feel like we are making a difference in a genuine, meaningful way.

You can be financially successful, a respected leader in your profession, be admired for your status, have beautiful possessions and a lovely family—but still feel a sense of emptiness and dull misery behind it all.

I find that most people who have made it in their career and have achieved success are feeling as I was that day on the porch many years ago. They have just about everything they want materially, but do not feel fulfilled. They want to venture out and make a difference, but are immobilized by fear and the need to have a familiar sense of security and stability. They also want to "fit in" to a society that values materialism and outward success over internal happiness. Yet what they are doing does not feel ultimately meaningful. The stability they hang onto often means their days are spent in routine and boredom. It becomes an exercise of just getting by day to day. Security often means that they do not take risks or allow themselves to be open to new possibilities. Many have lost the concept of having "enough" and cannot accept the idea of making less money for a while, even if it makes them happier. They cannot escape the money trap and therefore are not free. They feel like their lives are largely meaningless and they are wasting their time.

Because of the overwhelming need for survival, even beyond the point of enough, we ignore our deepest yearnings and continue in a job that is not fulfilling—or even worse, a job that is sapping our lifeblood and essence. We think we are making a living, but in reality our spirit is slowly dying.

An important turning point for me was when I had decided to leave a significant marketing position at a Fortune 500 company, but didn't know what to do next. I felt completely burned out with my profession but didn't see a way to make a transition into another career. In my mind, I was trapped by my "success" and couldn't envision taking a step "backward."

I felt completely stymied and boxed in since marketing for major corporations was all I had ever known. I had a heart-to-heart conversation with my ex-husband and he gave me some of the best advice I have ever received. He said: "Valerie, you can make half of what you are making now and still get by. You can pay your bills. Give yourself permission to explore, try something different. If you do what you love, you'll be great at it. And if you're great at it, success will come. In a few years you'll be making good money again."

This was some of the most liberating advice I have ever received. Right then and there, I made the commitment to be willing to make half of what I was making for one year (and then re-evaluate) in order to explore different options. The decision was totally liberating. I felt like I broke the chains that were keeping me immobile and sapping my spirit. And it opened up an exciting, new chapter in my life.

A JOB VS. YOUR LIFE'S WORK

Our single most important responsibility in life is to figure out what we came here to do. It is to find our life's work. We are disenchanted when we are simply working in a job. That's because there's a clear difference between money and joy.

In your job, money and joy are separate. You may find parts of your job that bring you joy, but your driving motivator is distinctly different—namely to get a paycheck and/or the perks that go along with it. In your life's work, money and joy coexist. You are, first and foremost, excited about your work.

People who achieve their Professional Destiny have a healthy attitude about money. They realize that the best things about money are that it gives options and that it can be used for good.

Many people find themselves bored and disillusioned simply because they never give serious consideration to what they'd really like to do in their profession; they continue to work in what they consider to be just a job, and have consistently prioritized other things higher in their life. It is a minority of people who choose to spend their lives in pursuit of objectives that are wholly worthwhile and bigger than they are. Feeling that nothing is worthwhile is what makes people feel disenchanted and unhappy.

Sometimes all it takes is an expanded perspective to find a way to contribute in a manner that satisfies your need to make even a small impact in your current profession. You may work in a company that does not currently match all of your ideals and needs guidance. You can provide that guidance. You can mentor others, especially if the leadership is receptive. Oftentimes what we think is a small contribution can have a greater impact than we imagine—and who knows, maybe your act of demonstrating by example may catch on.

If you start on the path to your destiny, you come into the flow of your life. You fall out of flow with the Universe if you renege on your path, or settle for safety, comfort and a mediocre life. Nonfulfillment, or disenchantment, is the opposite of fulfillment. It comes from failing to engage with your destiny. When you give up your dream, the world becomes a disillusioned place and you fall into the oblivion of non-realization. When you lose the flow, your life begins to lack meaning and purpose and becomes wearingly routine. You start to feel like you are living a life of silent desperation. In essence, you are mourning your unlived life.

Harold Kushner, Rabbi Laureate of Temple Israel in Natick, Massachusetts and author of several books, has said:

> "I believe that it is not dying that people are afraid of, it's something else.
>
> Something more unsettling and more tragic than dying frightens us. We're afraid of never having lived. Of coming to the end of our days with the sense that we were never really alive. That we never figured out what life was for."

Numerous studies have shown that having a purpose, or a feeling that you have realized meaning in your life, has a positive correlation to feelings of good health and well-being in the elderly. These findings were based on interviews with people 60 years and older who lived in community dwellings such as retirement homes. Interestingly, the regression analysis of one study also showed that purpose, even more than specific religious orientation, had a greater effect on feelings of well-being.

Conversely, feelings of living a life void of meaning led to the greatest sense of hopelessness and helplessness in the elderly. Not having a sense of purpose ranked highest as the primary source of depression, and even suicidal tendencies among this age group. The study conclusions strongly support the importance of meaning in life to a sense of satisfaction and well-being later in life.

We intuitively know there is a higher purpose for our existence. Whether we heed this call or not is a measure of our satisfaction throughout our lifetime. Living with purpose is our best insurance for feeling vital and satisfied in our golden years.

4

SELF-AWARENESS—YOUR GIFT, SKILLS & THE SCHOOL OF HARD KNOCKS

What you must dare is to be yourself.

—Dag Hammarskjold

Self-awareness is the first important step to discovering your gift. It is a time for introspection and a candid assessment of your strengths. Notice any interests you have or remember yearnings you felt at an early age. Identify times when you find yourself drawn to certain activities and notice when others seem to drain you. The following diagram points out the three elements that are critical to becoming a master at what you do.

A gift is something you are naturally good at. You are born with it. You can still become good at something else even if it is not your gift, but it takes more time and effort. Most likely you can become good enough, but not a master. In other words, you can become competent, but it will not be your Professional Destiny.

Skills and experience are acquired throughout your lifetime. A common misperception in the business world is that educational excellence is the be-all and end-all. An MBA gives you training and skills, but it does not provide you with your gift and it doesn't even necessarily identify what your gift is.

Many organizations make the mistake of hiring because of "credentials." They are considering only one or two sides of the triangle. For example, a Harvard MBA looks really good on a resume, but it first and foremost represents an indicator of skills. It is not necessarily an indicator of a gift, other than above-average intelligence. The degree itself is no guarantee that the person is capable of visionary ideas and causing breakthrough shifts in his or her profession. You can acquire a skill, but it will not cover for lack of a gift.

My proposition (sometimes unpopular) is that many people go on to get their advanced degrees because they haven't yet discovered their gift. While not entirely true, and certainly a profession like medicine or science is an exception, I often cite a powerhouse high-tech example to make this point.

What do Bill Gates, Michael Dell and Steve Jobs all have in common besides being CEOs of powerful technology companies? Each and every one had a strong vision; each dropped out of college and began pursuing his dream, seemingly with a great impatience. They had the gift, and developed the skills through the school of hard knocks—real life experience.

THE VISIONARY AND THE MASTER OF OPERATIONS

Where are you comfortable in your work? What type of leader are you? Do you consider yourself a great strategist looking into the future, or do you prefer to perfect things and make them hum? Here are definitions of two common types of leaders:

Visionary	Master of Operations
Sees potential	Takes the vision and makes things happen
Sees the future	Turns ideas into hard and fast reality
Knows what to do next	Knows what to do now
Great strategist	Great operationally
Sets and drives the vision	Shows results
Likes to build from scratch	More comfortable growing an existing idea, rather than developing one from scratch
Has little patience for process and day-to-day operations; is drained by them	Likes analysis and best practices, and thrives establishing process and operations
Is the inventor who steers the organization in new directions	Is the glue that holds the organization together and allows it to sustainably prosper

For any company to reach beyond a certain size, it needs both of these types at the top as well as leading each major department or initiative.

A *Visionary* typically starts an organization, takes it to a certain size, and then confusion and chaos tend to creep in. At this time he or she must find the *Master of Operations* to get to the next level.

Not all people who are pursuing their purpose will be out in the forefront leading the charge. In many of my consulting sessions, I worked with people in the top of their organizations to help them determine if they were a Visionary or a Master of Operations.

A Visionary is often the person who starts the organization and for this purpose, let's assume becomes the CEO. This person often is the futuristic leader and the big-picture thinker. Sometimes a Master of Operations starts an organization and can thrive to a certain level, but typically the idea behind the company already exists. A franchise is a good example—the idea for the business is already established, but a strong operational person can make it successful. The Master of Operations is the person best suited to run day-to-day operations. They are detail- and process-oriented and have the gift of getting things done. Rarely is a person a strong Visionary *and* Master of Operations, yet both are necessary as an organization expands. An organization that has a strong Visionary and Master of Operations often experiences a great deal of growth. Ironically, a common mistake that these organizations make is to believe that the two roles can be interchanged. When the Visionary retires or steps down, the Master of Operations who has been "groomed" often steps in to take his or her place. This rarely works because the Master of Operations cannot be taught to be the Visionary. It is not his or her gift. Similarly, a true Visionary rarely has the patience, interest and discipline for everyday details to keep the company on track.

In a leadership role, it's important to make an assessment of the best way for you to contribute. Both skills are essential. Do you initiate the vision or operationalize the vision that would not take off without you?

Extreme skills are not desirable without a complementary counter balance. For example, it is not ideal to be 100% visionary or 100% operational. A 100% visionary person can dream of things all day long but may not have the discipline to get anything done. On the other hand, someone who is 100% operational may get things done, but might not be able to see where to head next. It is best to create and encourage a synergistic partnership. The higher either percentage is in one individual, the more the complementary skill set is necessary. For example, a person who is 80% visionary and 20% operational must be paired with a highly operational person to achieve the greatest level of success. The higher the visionary percentage, the more brilliantly gifted this person is at seeing potential, but also the more important it is that he or she has operational support. This is a blind spot for the individual. On the other hand, a person with a 50/50 blend of operations and vision is often well-equipped to run a business or division on his/her own, but the visionary concept that starts the company might be more "normal" as opposed to ground-breaking and "genius." The business may be exceptionally successful and prosperous though.

If you fall into the highly visionary category, you like to think of things and start them from scratch. You thrive on creating new ideas, "seeing the big picture" and envisioning the possibilities. If you reflect back, your very best career accomplishments were when you operated in this capacity. Once the idea takes hold and turns into something that needs to become operationalized and repeatable, it is best to hand it off. The sooner the better.

If it stays with you, it will likely end up at the bottom of your priority pile, where things that are not all that interesting to you reside and only get done when someone is about to complain.

Someone else can take it and run with it. It's better that they do. You can think of the idea or direction, when perhaps they can't. But they can make it happen much better than you can.

Long-term, you will only be motivated if you are doing something you want to do and can see yourself happily sustaining the role. If you have ever found yourself in a position that asked you to be something you are not, you know how this feels. You become de-energized and deflated, and oftentimes you cease to be successful as you become less enthusiastic about your role.

Several years ago, I was in a marketing position where I was required to be less strategic and more operational. The company strategy of offering industry-standard products at low prices was set early on by the CEO, and up to that point it had been wildly successful. As the head of marketing for the business unit, I was asked to simply execute on this operational model. To thrive in that environment required memorizing sales numbers and operational dashboards on a daily basis and making adjustments to a model that already existed. If market share was low, we monitored the competition and product margins, and lowered the price. After a while, I found myself bored and de-energized. Others were happy with it, but I wasn't. As this happened, I found I couldn't fake my interest any more. This began the downward spiral—I went from being identified as a "high potential" employee in the top 10% of the company to someone who could barely drag herself into the office. It was time for me to move on to something else.

A NUDGE TO CHANGE

Once the soul awakens, the search begins and you can
never go back. From then on you are inflamed with a special
longing that will never let you linger in the lowlands of
complacency and partial fulfillment. The eternal makes you urgent.

—John O'Donohue

I spent over twenty years in the marketing profession and for much of it, I felt that I had found my gift. I used to say, "I'm a marketer through and through. Marketing is in my blood." I was successful at a young age and I quickly progressed up the ranks, becoming an executive at two Fortune 500 companies, starting my own business as a consultant and later becoming president of a nationally recognized advertising agency.

By all outward measures I had achieved success, my income was in the top 5% of the U.S. and my resume had grown to be impressive. Increasingly, though, I knew there was something "bigger" out there for me, and this time I wasn't focusing on the career ladder and finances alone. I knew I was meant to do something else. To be honest, it was quite disconcerting because my current situation provided for me and my family in a very comfortable, socially desirable and acceptable way. Yet, my current role no longer fulfilled me and I was rapidly losing interest. Out of integrity, I was beginning to feel like a fraud coming to work every day. Increasingly I couldn't ignore the message I was getting—and the more I looked for guidance through reflection, reading and coaching, the stronger the message came. I had a growing urge to do something meaningful, to give something back to the world, but I didn't know what this was. I didn't even know what I was interested in.

I just knew that I had to nurture the message growing in me. I recognized that I was given many gifts and I had an obligation in this lifetime to make use of them. What a waste it would be to look back at the end of my life and realize I had been given so much, compared to others who were truly struggling for survival, and I wasted the opportunity. I realized that I needed to get "on it" and figure out how to make a real contribution in a more meaningful way without further excuse and procrastination. Somehow I had to give back to others and experience a true sense of fulfillment. I could no longer focus solely on outward accomplishments, which really weren't making me happy anyway. That era was over.

For several months I had a sense that I should travel to India with the Miracle Foundation—a non-profit organization supporting orphans that was founded by my friend, Caroline Boudreaux, a few years earlier. Caroline had invited me on the trip as a volunteer for two years in a row, but I was always afraid to go and experience India's poverty first-hand—so I came up with some great excuses. Finally, another friend told me he was going and I decided the stars were lining up for me to do it. After the travel arrangements were made, he had to cancel and I was left to overcome my great fear of traveling alone to India, staying overnight and making a flight connection to a remote location before meeting up with the group. By this time, I had a strong sense that I simply had to go, so I sucked it up and got on the plane.

The first day, I was completely taken out of my element and appalled by all the chaos, poverty and dirt around me. I wanted nothing more than to be back home. Once I met up with the group and went to the orphanage, though, everything changed. I was greeted by over a hundred happy and healthy orphans.

Little boys shook my hand and asked "how do you do?" in formal, practiced English. Little girls grabbed my hands to walk with me, and everywhere we saw a sea of beaming faces. Soon I had an entourage of children following me around. I felt like a mother duck surrounded by all of her beautiful ducklings. It was joyous.

I experienced the children starting their day together very early with prayer, having breakfast, doing their chores and going to school. They wore handmade clothes, had only a shoebox-sized container for their meager belongings, yet shared every gift they received. I gave six girls some inexpensive, colorful barrettes that I had brought with me and they wore them proudly, showing them off every moment they could. The next day, I was surprised to see six different girls happily wearing them—to the delight of the girls who had given them. These kids had *nothing*, yet they were thrilled to share with each other. I found these children to be completely radiant human beings, and I was transformed through my experience with them.

I learned a valuable lesson on that trip—*you can't give without receiving.* I thought that I was the giver to the orphans, but I am quite certain that I was the receiver of the greater gift—these "untouchable" Indian orphans opened my heart and replenished my soul. I thought that if they could manage to be happy with so little, I, having so much more, could afford to take a risk and venture into another career. There was no doubt that my life, and perspective, had changed.

TAKING INVENTORY

So we've made the decision and reached the point of no return. Now what? What do we do? From my experience I have found the best answer is to take inventory of our strengths—what we are naturally good at and what we love to do. Then look for a theme.

Start by writing a list with three columns:

What I Love To Do

What I Am Good At

What I Loathe To Do

In the first two columns (*Love To Do* and *Good At*), be sure to include things such as "giving advice" or "nurturing" that are not necessarily recognized job skills. Here are some suggestions for you to make this exercise successful:

- Under the *Good At* column, list the skills and experience you already possess. Under the *Love To Do* section include things that continuously interest you, things you read or study in your spare time. Include the fields that interest you (nursing, the environment, teaching, chemistry, etc.). Capture anything that fascinates you, makes you feel energized or causes you to lose track of time.

- List everything you know about yourself. Also put everything you have heard about yourself in feedback from others (employee reviews, personality/career assessments) but only if you agree and believe them to be true.

- Define what you want to accomplish, what you want to do in your life and what you have to offer, in terms of your favorite gifts, skills and experience.

- Note your style of doing things—how you think, how you like to work, how you interact with others, what environments you like to be in (nurturing, logical, intuitive, detail-oriented, dynamic, creative).

- If you have skills that you are good at, you generally enjoy doing them. And if you enjoy doing them, you are usually good at them. This is typically, but not always, the case. So pay special attention to those interests/traits that make both sides of the list.

- If you have an impulse to put something on your list, include it.

In the third column (*Loathe To Do*), include the things that drain your energy and you want to avoid. Interestingly, you may or may not be good at them—but if you dread the thought of spending your time this way—write them down.

If you do this exercise and pay close attention, you will notice that you do know the things that you love and what you are uniquely good at. You just need to let this awareness surface and become top-of-mind. Make connections between what you're good at and what you love to do, and you will be better prepared to understand the kind of work you're best suited for in the future. Ask yourself, "what things must I have in my career to be fulfilled?" Promise to include them in your next choice. Then ask yourself "what things must I *not* have in my profession?"—and promise yourself to forever leave them behind.

People who get stuck (either temporarily or permanently) in this undertaking, get stuck because they do not pause, they do not reflect, they do not take the time to go within and know themselves.

Knowledge about yourself is a huge shortcut to traveling faster on your path. It will also keep you from getting off track, or overwhelmed by choices. Once you have this knowledge, put it into action—it prepares you to be truly extraordinary and is a critical step to identifying your Professional Destiny.

A few years ago, I determined that it was time to practice what I preach and take inventory of my own gifts. To further illustrate how this process works, the chart that follows shows how my own exercise turned out.

Note that I have italicized the skills that are common between the columns *Love To Do* and *Naturally Good At*:

Love To Do	Naturally Good At	Loathe To Do
Business and personal advising	Knowing people's strengths	Repetitive work
Working with people	Using intuition to read situations and people	Exist in a defined system with too much structure
Reading	Business acumen/ negotiation	Give up privacy/always have to be "on"
Writing	*Writing*	Take orders
Talking to people about their aspirations, the fundamental issues of living and their personal/ professional growth	Marketing	Day-to-day operations
	Taking a message and making it simple	Sit in long meetings
Leadership/building teams	*Leadership/building teams*	
Strategic thinking/seeing the big picture	*Strategic thinking/seeing the big picture*	
One-on-one communications	*One-on-one communications*	
Understanding what makes people tick	Individual and team motivation	
Creating messages that are clear, compelling and understandable	*Creating messages that are clear, compelling and understandable*	
Motivating people to reach goals	Being credible	
Helping people foster their creativity	Staying calm and fair	
	Empowering strong leaders/ individual contributors	
Building organizations where people recognize and practice their gifts	Dealing with ambiguity	
Thinking out of the box	Attention to detail at critical junctures	

From this, I dreamed up a career of consulting with people, drawing upon my marketing and business experience, and writing. If I could do this I would make full use of my gifts, interests, skills and experience, and never feel like I was working.

My vision was to write a book that would reach a mass audience so that I might help others, and use these same principles in my own work. I wanted to support, or create, an environment where people could thrive.

To reach your vision, it helps to become crystal clear on what is important to you. The best way to do this is to formulate three to five commitments (not too many so you can remember them) that will drive your decisions going forward. These must be things you feel strongly about and will hold fast to.

Here are the three commitments I came up with to support my vision for my career:

Fulfillment. I vowed that anything I did from now on in my career would have to be fulfilling. It would have to be matched with my strengths and interests. I would not take a job purely for money or title.

Abundance. I committed to make enough money to support myself and my family in a comfortable way and to help others do the same.

Service. Anything I did would have to contribute something meaningful to as many people as possible. I wanted to help people become aligned with their gifts and realize their full potential.

It is interesting how this journey has played out. First, I became a consultant and professional coach, and wrote this book. Next, I took an opportunity to go back into the advertising environment and was tasked with building an office from zero to over 200 people. I saw it as a chance to put all of my gifts, skills and experience into practice. I wanted to help build an organization where people recognize and practice their gifts. Where they would thrive. In hindsight, the experience gave me more perspective of what works and what doesn't—and the importance of alignment of vision among the leadership team. If you have alignment, great things can happen. If you don't, it's best to move on. Every experience is part of the journey and if you keep your vision and commitment in focus, you'll find that the people you met and the experiences you had better prepare you for the place you are in today.

Here are some guidelines for making commitments:

- Think carefully before you make commitments. Only make those with which you feel a strong connection and that you intend to keep. Commitments that you make anyway, but are unimportant to you, only encumber you in the long run.

- Write your vision and commitments down. There will be times when things get confusing and you'll want to go back and refresh your memory.

- Scrupulously evaluate all new opportunities against your commitments and don't waiver.

Setting your vision and making commitments sets up an agreement between you and the universe, and you'll more clearly recognize the opportunities that show up for you. If you go against these agreements, you break the bond and may quickly find yourself swimming upstream.

One of the most challenging questions I have asked, and often get asked, is this:

How do I set my vision if I don't know what it is? If I don't know what I want? The answer is to go within.

5

INTUITION—YOUR GREATEST GUIDE

The intuitive mind will tell the thinking mind
where to look next.

—Dr. Jonas Salk

Built into every human being is a perfect navigation system. Deep down you do know what you want. You have the answer, but sometimes it is harder to see because it is hidden beneath other priorities. We all have intuition, and if we quiet down and learn to tune in, we can train ourselves to hear it. Intuition is a sense above the intellect. It is a deep, inexplicable knowing that happens in the moment. Flashes of intuition are instantaneous, instinctive and fleeting. You cannot break intuition down, or predict or plan it, but you can learn to recognize it. If you pay attention, the signal will get stronger with time.

Some people keep themselves so busy that they can't hear their inner voice and have only slight access to their intuition. Many convince themselves that being busy is a sign of importance. Oftentimes they are running because they've forgotten about their greatest guide, they don't trust that it can lead them or simply don't want to hear what it has to say.

Many of us learn at an early age to tune out our inner voice and we choose to focus on survival. It may be because we are ridiculed or it may be that it doesn't seem practical, but in the long run the costs of this are high.

We have two strong pulls inside of us—to be self-sufficient, independent and free; and to be part of something larger and meaningfully involved with other people.

Intuition teaches us from within. It is our unerring guide. In our heart there is the hint of the next step. You must remain attentive and receptive to all possibilities, even possibilities that don't seem logical to you at the moment. It may be something simple, such as making a phone call or having the idea to set up an appointment with someone. Intuition is a great tool in your profession and in your life. It will give you a sense of who you can trust, who is ethical, who has your best interests at heart and who you should avoid altogether.

In the workplace, intuition is especially useful for making all-important employee hiring decisions, or for choosing a business partner. For example, during the interviewing process some people are polished interviewers and present themselves well, but then turn out to be much less impressive when they're on the job. Others are less polished, but you have an inexplicable sense they will be great contributors on a day-to-day basis. Often it all comes down to your intuition. After making a hiring mistake early in my management career, I learned to hone my intuition during the process and pay attention to my gut feelings. I developed what I called "my lower left corner" interviewing process. I took notes throughout the interview and would record the answers to my questions on a sheet of paper in front of me for future reference but in the lower left corner I would record my "impressions"—whatever struck me during the interview. I might be interviewing a perfectly polished individual and get the feeling that he is "cocky" and that would go in the corner. Or I might be interviewing someone who says all the right things but can't make eye contact with certain questions and I record that as a warning sign.

On the other hand, I may be interviewing someone who is a little nervous, but who I can tell has high integrity and a strong work ethic. I record that in the lower left corner too. After the interview, I weigh my intuition along with the candidate's answers and experience. If I suspect a possible flaw, I ask myself if it is something we could live with. For example, I may get the feeling that someone will be nervous giving a presentation and then decide that it is okay in this position because someone else will be the public face. Often that is a livable weakness. If the "flaw" that I suspect is of someone's character or integrity, however, I will not overlook it, no matter what the qualifications or how urgently I need to fill the position. It always comes back to bite you. When I have gone back and compared my "lower left corner" notes to my perceptions of people six months after they are hired, I have found them to be almost always accurate. In fact, it wasn't that I didn't intuit the weakness accurately, the only unpredictable variable seemed to be my judgement of how much, or how little, that "weakness" would impact the person's performance in that particular role.

In terms of our purpose, it's not that we don't know what it is. It's that we've forgotten how to listen to ourselves so that it might become more clear. We don't know how to tap into it because it's become so disguised by our fears and the external expectations—proper social standing, education and career—that we feel compelled to live up to.

You must get quiet and go within to get centered. Do this

in order to make the right choices and stay committed to finding your purpose, to finding your calling.

How do you know when you go off the path or go against yourself?

When you go against your inner voice and consequently your destiny, you will start to feel uncomfortable. The more aware you are and the further down your path, the greater the discomfort becomes. It can be a physical symptom at your usual stress point in your body (your back goes out, you get a headache, your face goes numb) or a deep-seated feeling of depression. It is an indication that "You" (your soul) know your path and that you (your persona) are ignoring it. It is different than the everyday worries that preoccupy you. It is very deep and pervasive.

We have all had this experience of going against ourselves. We might have ignored it or kept ourselves so busy that we were hardly even aware of it, but it has been there. Sometimes we don't like the direction it's pointing because it is leading us into unknown territory or requires a change to the life that, for better or worse, we've grown accustomed to. But this intuition, this inner knowing, is our greatest guide. If we acknowledge it, we will become increasingly aware and its voice will seem louder. It can show us the direction we should head.

If you ignore your guidance, it may become urgent and painful. Even if you pretend not to hear what it tells you, it will always be there inside you, nudging you with a sense of discomfort and trying to get you to listen. Sometimes when you are completely closed off it will recede to another time when you are more receptive to hearing it.

6

DUELING FORCES

People with high levels of mastery…
cannot afford to choose between reason and intuition,
or head and heart, any more than they would choose
to walk on one leg or see with one eye.

—Peter Senge

The duel between reason and intuition, or head and heart, is a constant and powerful force in our lives.

Head—also known as our mind. It is the home of our rational thought and logic. Our drive for survival.

Heart—also known as the soul, spirit or essence. It is the home of our intuition (some also call it our "gut"). It is the home of our higher self and represents who we really are at the core.

HEAD VS. HEART

Head	Heart
Voice of reason	Inner voice
Rationality	Intuition
Logic	Soul
Survival	Spirit
Experience	Possibilities
Persona/Personality	Essence

Achieving stature and safety in life serves to satisfy and comfort the mind. At some point, if we are committed to a path of purpose, we will experience an insurgency of the soul—an insistent demand that we live more consciously and meaningfully. Our job is to stay focused on this deeper message, so that we can call it forth reliably and use its guidance to steer ourselves in a more satisfying direction.

The moment we stop learning is the moment we begin to stagnate. We go to sleep and our life becomes empty with an unsettling combination of anxiety and boredom.

Once you start on your journey and follow your deepest yearning, you won't be able to turn back and keep it quiet. Human beings are born learning and growing. Even if you keep yourself so busy and pretend not to hear it, you will feel a deep sense of dissatisfaction and experience disenchantment with your life. Your inner voice will always be there, even if buried, waiting for you to listen.

PERSONALITY VS. SOUL

Sometimes people carry to such perfection
the mask they have assumed that in due course
they actually become the person they seem.

—W. Somerset Maugham, *The Moon and Sixpence*

The word *personality* comes from *persona*; which is the Latin word for mask. It is the outer self that we present to the world, the mask that we wear to survive. Our personality is a reflection of our outer world: the religion we are raised with, our education, our career, the level of success we achieve, our looks, how fit we are, our friends. Our soul is our inner world. It is our essence. It knows our destiny and our purpose and lives underneath the mask. In a sense our personality is shaped like a character in a play—a mask that's presented to the world with the real person inside.

Carl Jung refers to the concept of *individuation*, the process in which a person discovers and evolves his Self, as opposed to his ego. The ego is a persona, a mask worn in everyday social interaction. The Self, on the other hand, is our true center, our awareness of ourselves without outside influence and interference.

When they are young, almost all people have an inkling of what their destiny is. They are dreamers, full of enthusiasm and everything seems possible. They do not accept "no" and they have not yet been biased by what other people think. The problem is that as they get older, they begin to think more about what is expected of them and they become preoccupied with wearing the correct mask, rather than what they truly want for themselves. When we become outwardly focused instead of inwardly focused, there is nothing holding us back more than ourselves.

The struggle between our personality and our soul, especially when we are confronting deep-seated, oftentimes irrational fears of survival, can be vicious and potentially debilitating if it spins out of control.

For example, immediately after I had finished the exercise of figuring out what I loved to do, what I was good at and setting my commitments, I found myself confronted by limiting thoughts and the small, critical voice inside me. It told me that I would never make another penny after I left my high-profile job and pursued writing my book. Worse, it said I would never get published, no one would pay for my type of consulting, I would have to sell my house, my colleagues would think I'd had a mid-life crisis and my life, as well as my bank account, would slowly but surely evaporate into nothingness.

Here are some of the questions that my nasty inner critic asked me:

Who do you think you are anyway?

What makes you think "you" can do this?

Do you realize how embarrassed you'll be when this fails?

How old are you anyway? Shouldn't you have started this years ago? It's too late now.

What if no one buys your book?

What if everyone thinks it's stupid?

What if everyone thinks *you're* stupid?

What makes you think you can be successful starting a business and altering your career? Most people fail.

Do you have a clue how to get published? No. How are you going to do it then? It's almost impossible.

Have you lost all sense?

This is the end of your career. You're never going to make another penny. How are you going to support yourself?

How are you going to support your family?

How are you going to survive?

This is called the "little voice" inside you. The internal critic. It lives in your mind and it is mean! You do not need to pay attention to any voice that makes you feel stupid, incompetent and fearful. It comes from your lower self—the self that keeps you limited. Your "little voice" is quite distinct, and the opposite, of the true "inner voice" that comes from intuition. Your inner voice has a completely different tone—it's much calmer, quieter and friendlier. It always points you in the right direction. If you listen with awareness, you can learn to distinguish between the two.

Pay attention to your inner voice and stay focused on your vision, and your little voice will eventually quiet down from lack of attention. Simply tell it, "thanks for sharing, but I'm going to do this instead" and continue on your way.

Fortunately, as my little voice was taking center stage and I was considering "selling out," I discussed a lucrative job offer that I was considering—but didn't really want—with my daughter. She said: "Mom, you are writing a book about doing what you are meant to do. Don't you think you should practice what you preach?" She stopped me in my tracks. What could I say to that? Nothing. She reminded me of my vision and gave me the nudge I needed to recommit. I renewed my vow to have courage, turn down the "safe" job offer and stick to my guns. Nevertheless, four months into the process, I found myself facing some of my deepest fears about survival, having panic attacks about finances and suffering from severe migraines. Once I realized that my fears were making me sick, I recalibrated and stepped back onto my path. I figured if I was going to go down, I might as well go down healthy (instead of in bed draining my bank account by being debilitated and poisoning my body with every type of costly migraine medication I could find) and pursue my dream. At that moment I made a deal with the Universe that I would absolutely pursue a career doing what I loved to do and see what happened. Once I made that commitment, things began to fall in place. The faintest stirrings of momentum began.

THE KILLER COMBO

It took me several years to learn a great secret: the magic of the word "and." Always before, I thought of things as "or"—Head or Heart, Money or Happiness, Survive or Thrive, and so on. In these situations, when you realize that "and" is far more empowering than "or," you come up with "the killer combo."

We are given the gifts of rationality (head) and intuition (heart); of the outward facade we present to the world (personality) and our inner essence (soul). In each case, the former helps us with survival in the physical world we live in, the latter allows us to have breakthroughs that are genuine, unique and fresh. In terms of discovering your purpose, finding harmony in the combination of Head/Heart and Personality/Soul is the most powerful mix.

THE WALNUT

What would a shriveled heart look like? Someone who's completely lost touch with their higher meaning? After watching *How the Grinch Stole Christmas,* by Doctor Seuss, on TV when I was very young, I got the idea that someone who lost touch with their higher meaning would look like the Grinch, and a shriveled heart would look like a walnut.

The Grinch had become a bitter, miserable creature who was clearly cut off from his inner voice and any kind of satisfying purpose in life. In fact he was so low, he couldn't stand seeing others having a happy or meaningful life. He looked shriveled and bitter, with no light in his eyes. The Grinch *hated* Christmas. Why? No one knew exactly, but according to the story, the most likely reason was that his heart was two sizes too small.

Some people's hearts get so closed down through their hurts, disappointments and negative experiences in life that their heart shrivels and contracts like a walnut. For some of us, it goes even further and a protective shell starts to form around that shriveled heart. The shell becomes hard, dark, brittle and difficult to penetrate. And when it gets too strong, it blocks all access to the heart and the person, like the Grinch, becomes, looks and acts... miserable.

You can see a shriveled heart through someone's eyes. All inner radiance is blocked. Their eyes are empty. They are not expressing their full potential.

There is a direct pathway from the heart to the eyes. I call this the "Heart-to-Head Expressway." If your heart is open and full, and the expressway is clear, you will show great vibrancy and radiance in your eyes. You will have a sense of aliveness, energy and creativity about you. If your heart is shriveled and contracted, and the expressway is blocked, your eyes will look empty and dull. Your life seems routine.

The Grinch's heart was so contracted and he was so miserable that in the middle of the night he dressed up as Santa Claus and stole all the presents, ribbons, decorations and wrappings. He escaped to his cave on the mountaintop before daybreak and anxiously awaited the moment that the Who's realized Christmas was ruined. Instead they came out singing. The Grinch simply *couldn't* figure this out. He stood puzzling until a new thought dawned on him—maybe Christmas held a deeper meaning. Maybe it meant more than gifts...

> "And what happened then...?
> Well... in Who-ville they say
> That the Grinch's small heart
> Grew three sizes that day!
> And the minute his heart didn't feel quite so tight,
> He whizzed with his load through the bright morning light
> And he brought back the toys! And the food for the feast!
> And he...
> ... HE HIMSELF...!
> The Grinch carved the roast beast!"
> —Dr. Seuss, *How the Grinch Stole Christmas*

In simple terms, you could say the Grinch got a crack in his walnut shell when he heard the Who's singing without any presents or material things. Once his shell was cracked, as he stood there puzzling, his heart could see the light of the true meaning of Christmas, and it suddenly plumped out and expanded three sizes. Best of all, once this happened the Grinch found his purpose—he stood at the head of the table surrounded by all the Who's and, looking very fulfilled, carved the roast beast!

7

CHOICE, ACTION & COMMITMENT

There is a vitality that is translated through you into action.
And because there is only one of you in all time, this expression
is unique, and if you block it, it will be lost. The world will not
have it. It is not your business to determine how good it is
nor how it compares with other expressions. It is your business
to, clearly and directly, keep the channel open.

—Martha Graham

Making a choice sets the forces of creation in motion. Security can be an illusion. When you don't have to cling to things that bring you greatness, you can participate more in what's directly in front of you. Then you experience what is happening instead of just thinking about it. Show up and see what happens.

CROSSING THE THRESHOLD AND TAKING ACTION

To venture causes anxiety,
but not to venture is to lose oneself.

—Soren Kierkegaard

We put one foot in front of the other and take one step at a time.

Jack Canfield makes a wonderful analogy in *The Secret*. It's about knowing your ultimate destination but only being able to see what is immediately in front of you. If you are in a car, driving from New York to Los Angeles in the dark, you only get to see the area lit up by your headlights directly in front of you—maybe 200 feet. If you want to see further, the only way to see the next 200 feet is to move forward. Even though you may be traveling 3,000 miles, if you have faith in your directions and believe that you will ultimately get there, you'll be fine just seeing 200 feet at a time. This analogy reminds us that we don't get to see the entire path to our destination; we just get to see a little at a time. If we keep the faith and keep going, we will see the next part of the journey, and then the next, until ultimately we arrive at our destination.

Take a step even if you can't see anything beyond it. Have faith that you will ultimately reach your destination and make a choice. Sometimes we think that not choosing will keep options open. In the short term this can be true, but it is never true for the long term. Ultimately not choosing weighs us down in inaction and confusion. Making a choice is a powerful first step, it sets the forces of creation in motion.

Take action.

When you are meant to be on your path to fulfilling your destiny, you will experience discomfort when you stall or take the wrong direction. Ignore a message or an opportunity, and next time it will come in louder and be more painful. How many of us have experienced this in the past when we were locked in an unfulfilling, unstimulating or unhealthy profession? We may start feeling that we are failing in our position, we may be left out of key meetings or we may be passed up for promotion. The pain just gets worse and worse until it becomes unbearable. We leave, or even worse, we become too afraid to leave. We sell out on our spirit and resign ourselves to a mediocre life.

Opportunity taps you on the shoulder; if you don't listen, it taps a little harder the next time to let you know it's serious and to get your attention. If you still don't listen, the next time it will knock you flat until you become so miserable, you *have* to do something.

It is a far more enjoyable life experience if you listen the first time and heed the message before it begins to hurt and knocks you flat.

Before you get to the next step, often you need to close the door on the current situation that is not working for you before you get to open another.

Another way to think of this is to imagine Tarzan swinging from vine to vine in the jungle. He can't move forward on a new vine, without letting go of the vine he was on. If he holds on to the old vine and doesn't grab the new one, he'll go backward. If he tries to hold both vines, he'll get stuck. He must let go of the old vine and grab the new one to ride forward to his destination.

When you are pursuing your purpose, you will need to be fiercely disciplined—but it is a discipline born of passion, not of fear. Being on your path will cause you profound moments of joy. You will feel alive, creative and committed, and you will know you're going in the right direction.

If your chosen path is causing your spirits to wither, it's a strong signal that you are headed in the wrong direction.

INTENTION, CREATING, IMAGING

Take a stand. This is an act of using language to create a new possibility. Some stands are as simple as saying "I will make one thing happen today." When you start with 100% conviction, it tends to set things in motion. Example of other stands you might say are: "today, I'll find the humor in every situation that comes my way" or "today, I will notice and appreciate every opportunity that knocks on my door, even if it's not what I expected." Taking a stand keeps you centered, focused and alert, and sets the tone for your day.

If you ask for success and simultaneously prepare for failure, you will get the situation you prepare for. For example, in my first year as a consultant after leaving my presidency role, I told myself that I was going to give myself a little break after twenty years of an intense career. I wanted to work for pay only part-time and spend the rest of my day writing and doing marketing for a non-profit organization. I considered it a year of vacation and replenishing my soul. My goal was simply to "break even" in my expenses for myself and my daughter, and I would cut costs by cutting all of the luxury items I would normally purchase (facials, pedicures, a new car after mine reached 100,000 miles, furniture to complete my living room, fun new clothes) in order to fund my freedom.

I called my savings my "freedom money" and guarded it fiercely. Instead of thinking about it as "lack," or not having enough money to buy these things, I thought of it as a choice. This was money I was investing in myself to fund my freedom. I figured out what amount was the bare minimum for me to live on and I put this number in my head. It was a fraction of my earnings for the five previous years, but it was the number that stuck with me. Later, I realized that amount was a little more "bare bones" than I really wanted to live on and I told myself that I should increase the number. I put a new number in my head but I could sense that I didn't completely believe it. To demonstrate this point, when my accountant asked me in April to project my earnings for the rest of the year, I gave him the lower number even though I was trying to convince myself that I would earn the higher number. If I were honest, deep down I felt that the lower number was okay and I accepted it even though I continued to unconvincingly hope for more. In essence, I was asking for success, but not fully believing it—and preparing for failure. In January of the following year when I was reviewing my income for the year, I realized that it was almost exactly (within $200) of the figure I had given my accountant eight months earlier. It made perfect sense that I made what I had originally asked for and truly believed in. In the end, it all turned out fine and I accomplished what I wanted for the year, but it was a clear example of getting what you truly envision and believe in.

This principle also applies in the positive sense. In your profession, decide what you are worth, put the number in your head, picture it and fully believe it. Hold your belief without wavering and see what happens. Sometimes a new opportunity presents itself that fulfills your goal, or sometimes you magically receive a promotion or salary increase where you are. I've seen many people experience these situations. You know when you believe it and it is non-negotiable. What we think, we create. A friend of mine who owns a young advertising agency was barely making ends meet for months. She said to me: "I couldn't really decide what to do with my agency and we weren't making it. So, I changed my mind (and decided what we were going to do and how much we needed to make), believed it and it worked."

Many years ago, I put a clear number in my head of what I decided I was worth that was almost twice as high as what I was making at the time. I believed it without a doubt, but didn't know how it would happen. Within two years I was making that amount. The trick is your belief. If you are honest with yourself and pay attention, you will know if you truly believe it or not. If you don't believe yourself, try to uncover the root of your feelings of lack, unworthiness or doubt. Maybe the shortfall is truly okay with you and that's why it's not happening, or maybe it isn't and you need to make a mental shift. What you end up getting is exactly what you expect and believe you will get.

Release yourself from old limiting beliefs that are keeping you stuck. Take a new stand for your self-worth. Keep declaring it to yourself and visualize it. We can only receive what we "see" ourselves receiving. This relates to our profession, our relationships, our income, our accomplishments. If we can't see it, but want to, we can ask another to hold the vision for us and help us see it. This can be a friend, a coach or anyone who has our best interests at heart. Sometimes we are too close to our own situation and we become doubtful or fearful. Our friend, however, can clearly see our gifts and opportunities, and never waiver because he or she is not close to the situation or blinded by fears and emotions. It is much easier to help someone else than yourself, so seek out help when you feel yourself wavering.

If you help another succeed, you ultimately help yourself

succeed. The true purpose of networking with others is not to go into it wondering what the other could do to aid you, but rather what you can do to help the other person. If you follow this approach, it is remarkable so see what begins to happen in your life. Good will produces great abundance and protection around the one who sends it.

The outcomes of your life show what you are visioning. If you are afraid to move forward, you may manifest a situation or illness that rationalizes your unconscious intention to stay stuck where you are. If you have pictured prosperity and reaching your goal, you are far more likely to make movement and manifest the success you are looking for.

Paint a picture in your mind. See yourself starting your journey with a smile on your face. You may face roadblocks now and then, but keep your vision in mind. Feel confident that you will eventually get there. The journey is invigorating and exciting. Use your imagination to paint the most believable picture you can—with the most realistic details—if you are an athlete, see yourself stumble, get up and run again. Then see yourself standing on the medal podium at the Olympics and feel for a moment the joy that you know you will feel.

FINDING HERSELF IN A PLACE SHE'D NEVER BEEN—
A FOUNDER'S STORY

Caroline Boudreaux is the founder of the Miracle Foundation—a non-profit organization that transforms the lives of orphans in India. She journeyed from a young, successful TV sales executive to the leader of a growing organization that has raised millions of dollars in funding, built ground-breaking new children's villages and has supported thousands of orphans and tsunami survivors. Here is her story:

"At age 28, I worked at a local TV station as an account executive selling TV spots. I was making more money than I had ever dreamed of, and yet was totally miserable. I had everything someone at my age could want... a beautiful condo, a new car, lots of money and many friends. I kept thinking once I get a boyfriend, once I get this, once I get that... I'll be happy. At that moment though, I was empty... a total hedonist, partying almost every night.

I said to myself, 'you look like you've made it, but inside you're miserable. You're not the girl you used to be. You've lost your spark. I *knew* that I had a purpose and that I wasn't fulfilling it. I was absolutely sure there had to be more to my life, but I didn't have a clue what I was supposed to be doing.

One night in March, I ended up face down on the floor bawling my eyes out. Out of desperation, I made a promise to God that I would do anything, at any cost, if He would just fill this emptiness I was feeling—this hole in my heart.

The promise I made didn't really change my behavior at first—I was still partying, but I spent some time reading the Bible, being open and listening to a very inspirational minister on tape.

In October, my friend Christine and I were sitting around at Happy Hour and we decided to take a pleasure trip around the world and get away. The goal was to chase summer for a full year. I was so sick of my job that I agreed to go.

One of the places Chris wanted to go was India. She had sponsored a little boy named Manus there through the Christian Children's Fund (CCF) and she wanted to see if he was real. I agreed and we started our journey around the world in January of 2000.

First we went to Bombay where things quickly became complicated and difficult. We had a hard time trying to find someone who could help us get to Manus. He lived in Choudwar in the state of Orissa and we couldn't find anyone who spoke the local language to communicate with them. On top of this, Chris was trying to quit smoking and was at the end of her patience. It was hot as hell (119 degrees). It was dirty and nasty, and getting very expensive. It was going to cost another $750 to get to Manus and we were on a budget of $50 per day (that meant 15 days of budget was gone). I remember sitting there in the travel agent's house in India watching her work and wondering if we were getting ripped off or if our money was actually going toward the trip.

Finally out of frustration Chris said, "Let's just send him the money—$1,500 and forget it."

I said, 'No, we've come this far… we're going.'

So, a few days later, after hours of Chris making arrangements for the trip from a pay phone, we flew to Bhubaneshwar where we were greeted at the airport with flowers by people from the CCF.

From there we met the Director of CCF, Papa. He was an amazing, boisterous man who loved to talk. And that day we went to meet Manus. Over 300 villagers welcomed us and paraded us through the village. A woman washed my feet and dried them with her dress and as she stepped aside, there was Manus. He was eight or nine years old and we were happy to discover that he had gotten everything Chris had ever sent—every picture, card and letter. We decided to stay for a while and volunteered in the village for nine days. On May 14th (Mother's Day) the director, Papa, invited us to dinner at his home. We drove up in the car and were instantly surrounded by 110 filthy, hungry orphans. We had dinner with Papa eating chicken and vegetables, and the children were fed rice with a little bit of sugar.

He told us the story of how 17 years ago, he had found a starving orphan in the field and had taken him home to live with his wife and children; then after a cyclone hit, he took in 14 others. Now they have 110. The government paid only $6 per month for the support of each child, which was not enough —and they were dying of preventable things like diarrhea.

After dinner, I picked up a little girl named Shebani. She literally pressed her skinny body into mine to get all the affection she could, fell asleep in my arms and then peed all over me. As I took her back to her room, I was met by a stench that could have taken down a grown man. The children slept on wooden beds much like picnic tables. As I laid Shebani down on those planks and heard her bones hit the wooden slats, I knew I had to do something. It was Mother's Day and that was the beginning of the Miracle Foundation.

After that night, I was so emotional. I told Chris that I could never go back there again. It was horrific seeing those children like that. It was jarring. Haunting.

Chris said, 'You can and you will. In this world, there are the givers and the receivers. You are so lucky to be able to be the giver.'

It was unfair.

Why were they born into that? They were starving and I was partying like a rock star. I was distraught. It was wrong. That experience at the orphanage changed everything and I could never go back to my life as it was. I found myself standing face to face with the truth.

We went back to the orphanage and the village a few times before moving on to our next stop and all I could think of was those kids. I was tormented. Chris told me, 'I want you to write down every way you can help those kids and when you can't think, think some more.' I'll never forget, I was at the top of the mountain in Nepal in a teahouse. I hiked four miles uphill, had tea and I'm writing and writing and crying and listening to Bob Marley.

Finally I wrote, 'Open an adoption agency,' and instantly felt relief. I said 'that's it!' It was a decision to take action and it started my journey.

It was hard work setting up an agency... filing for 501C3 status, getting licensed, advertising, etc. I visited an adoption agency in Houston and the joke was that the only reason they were successful was because no one told them they couldn't do it. They told me to be willing to work for ten years without results.

Driving home from Houston, I started thinking 'I don't think I can do this. There are 12.4 million orphans living in India. I'm only one person and the job is so big. I just don't think

I can do it.' I told God I would do it if He wanted me to, but I needed another sign.

I went home and there was a package on my doorstep. It was a framed picture of me surrounded by children in front of the orphanage. Chris had framed it and attached a message that she'd made with a label maker. Miraculously, it said:

'You can do it!'

It was my sign—clear as day. And I was going to go for it.

It took me three years and going through a lot of government red tape to open that agency. Still it seemed that the closer I got, the more problems I faced. I discovered that international adoption is riddled with corruption, and the more I learned about the ethical implications, the more I realized I was off track. I might help 20 children a year when there were millions that needed help. I worked until my money ran out.

In order to support myself during this time, I worked at a local advertising agency as a contract sales person. I had no success for 13 months. One day the truth hit me—I had no money, no sales and no results, and the Miracle Foundation wasn't moving either.

It was hell. It was awful. Then to top it off, at the same time all of this was happening, my boyfriend that I thought I was going to marry, broke up with me.

So, here I was, trying to do a good thing that I thought God wanted me to do, working my tail off and was not successful on any front... no money, no adoption agency, no sales, no man.

It was April, 2003. I had $4,000 left to my name and worse

I was waiting for another sale to pay the taxes I had made on the $200,000 I made the past year in television sales. I was anxious and terribly in debt!

Out of desperation, I began interviewing for a sales position at the local CBS affiliate, because I was scared and nothing was happening.

I remember sitting on the back porch, talking to my friend Charlotte, crying. I felt dead in the water. 'How come God would tell me to help the orphans and then won't let it work out? What kind of God puts you at an orphanage on Mother's Day and then doesn't let you help?'

She urged me to go to India one more time and made sure I immediately booked a trip. It took every bit of courage I had and cost me all the money I had left. I was terrified.

I went to India to see Papa. It was three years after that first Mother's Day and I had been sending whatever money I could. I realized on that trip that my plan needed to morph... adoptions were definitely not going to work. We decided to do a sponsorship program instead and he gave me 25 kids to start off with.

I came home in June 2003. I absolutely couldn't see at that time how it was going to work out, but somehow, I knew it was all going to come together. It would be okay. I had a peace about it (though that didn't make any sense). Later I realized that I always had faith, but I just didn't know what it was going to look like.

I met a man named Alan Graham, who ran the organization Mobile Loaves and Fishes, and he became my mentor. He asked me what my job was. I said 'my job is to help orphans. He then corrected me and said 'your job isn't to help orphans... your job is to find ways for *other* people to help orphans and allow them to fill the God-shaped hole in their hearts.'

These words changed everything. It was a turning point in my thinking and it meant I could ask for help. I suddenly felt comfortable.

I needed $3,600 a month to live and I was out of money. I did not know how I was going to get through the next month. Then miracles began to happen...

A few days later, one of the agencies I had previously worked for called me. They told me that one of the accounts I'd worked on had just given them a contract. This was an account I had given up the expectation that it would ever close. They told me that they were going to write me a check for $3,800. It got me through the month.

The next month, July, another client had an audit and discovered that they had underpaid me. They sent me a check for $3,600 and it was just enough to get me through another thirty days.

Then on the 28th of July, I was in the shower and I didn't know how I was going to get through the next month. I was scared. I said to God, "I don't have to do this. I can still take the job with CBS. It's the 28th... don't test me, Dude! I will go back to the corporate world. I don't have to do it!

That night I went to a prayer meeting. My friend had just started a family foundation and had adopted a boy from Romania. She told me 'My husband and I just founded a foundation' and handed me a check for $10,000. 'This is for you to live, not for the children.' It was the first check their foundation wrote.

Because of Alan Graham's advice and then this money, I was freed up. I held my first fundraiser in November and raised $75,000 in cash and pledges that night. It was the beginning of the Miracle Foundation as it is today."

8

MOVING THE BOULDER

*You may think that real work is doing your job,
but the real work is finding
what you are supposed to do with your life.*

—Oprah Winfrey

A friend and trusted advisor, Perch Ducote, described three important stages for the creation of your dream: Formulation, Concentration and Momentum. The example he cited was starting a new business.

He said, "Imagine a large boulder sitting right in front of you and you need to move it to get started with your business and on your path."

In the first stage, the formulation stage, you define your vision and become self-aware saying, "This is who I am, this is where I am going and this is what I'm about." You begin the creation process.

In the second stage, the concentration stage, you need to give a concentrated amount of energy to make it happen. It is a time to prove to the Universe that you are committed and that you mean what you say. It is about discipline. If you say you are going to make ten calls today, you make ten calls. When you don't feel like it, make the next one. You show confidence—you tell the world "watch out, I'm coming, don't mess with me. I am absolutely the right person to make this happen."

The concentration stage is no fun. It is when you start pushing the boulder and there is inertia—total resistance—at first. It hasn't moved for a long time, but you need to push it, drive it and not give up. You may feel like you are fighting the Universe because you put a lot more energy out than you get back. You're working hard, yet there are not a lot of results. It takes grit, determination, strength of will and persistence. You don't see much progress in the beginning, but you keep your shoulder to the boulder and keep pushing. You refuse to become a victim and insist "I will make this happen. I've got the power. I can do it." Eventually the boulder will budge and begin to move. Slowly at first. But keep pushing, concentrate on pushing.

In the third stage, the momentum stage, the boulder gradually begins to move a little easier. It generates momentum and begins to take on a life of its own. Things start happening and you begin seeing the fruits of your labor. At this point the boulder moves without much effort. The forward movement is exciting and motivating. You experience the beginnings of success. The secret to continued success, however, is to keep pushing—calling, networking and managing so that the boulder doesn't slow down and force you to overcome inertia again.

Taking this analogy a step further, the formulation stage is a time when you clearly set your vision and become focused intensely on self-awareness: taking stock of your strengths, your interests, what you are good at and what you are not. You focus on your gifts and develop skills and experience to get you to your ultimate goal.

You commit to being authentic with yourself, knowing yourself so completely that you become immune to self-deception. Then you get to the hard work…

DISCIPLINE

You have to find something that you love enough
to be able to take risks, jump over the hurdles,
and break through the brick walls that are always
going to be placed in front of you. If you don't
have that kind of feeling for what it is you're doing,
you'll stop at the first giant hurdle.

—George Lucas

What does discipline mean when it comes to achieving your vision? It means reminding yourself of your vision every day and committing yourself to the straightest, most direct path to get from here to there. It means shedding everything that is holding you back as soon as you become aware of it.

Discipline means that after you set your vision, you prepare for your journey, set your commitments and push through all of the obstacles that are thrown in your way. Your vision must be strong to inspire you when the going gets tough, and you must have discipline to find the courage to take a step toward your dream, even on the lowest, most miserable of days.

The next story is about discipline, persistence and overcoming incredible odds to pursue a childhood professional dream…

BULLIED TO BESTSELLER—AN AUTHOR'S STORY

Trevor Romain is a noted children's author and illustrator, video personality and public speaker. His more than thirty published books have over a million copies in print, many translated into 14 languages. He is well known for his work in the community as a board member of the National Candlelighters Childhood Cancer Foundation, and has worked closely with the Make-A-Wish Foundation and Miracle Foundation.

Over the years Trevor has spoken at hundreds of elementary, middle and high schools across the United States on topics such as homework, stress, taking care of your body, facing fears and dealing with grief. Trevor is also featured as a keynote speaker at medical, educational and corporate conferences. Here is his story:

"My childhood was not picture perfect. I was in special education in school, I was dyslexic, I was considered the dunce and I was often bullied at school.

When I was eight years old I remember walking past a book store with my dad and in the bookstore were the original Winnie-the-Pooh books, not the Disney version, but the ones with the beautiful line-drawing illustrations by EH Shepherd. I said to my dad, 'when I grow up, I want to write a book just like that.' And he said to me, 'why wait till then, why don't you do it now?'

So I started writing stories. Badly at first, because I couldn't spell due to my dyslexia, but I was so passionate about the books and I loved the sketches. I always wanted to write from that time. I also wanted to illustrate my own books. The road there wasn't easy. I remember my teachers telling my father that if I would only stop dreaming I might get somewhere in my life. But in reality, dreams are what got me where I am today.

When I was 12 years old, I went to high school and applied to Mr. Ulrich Lowe's art class. He wrote a letter to my dad that said something to the effect of: 'Dear Mr. Romain, we regret to inform you that your son isn't talented enough to do art.' So I then went through high school drawing in the margins of my book, which I got spanked for. And then I tried to go to art college but I didn't have a portfolio and they told me I wasn't talented enough, so I stopped drawing and didn't draw again for 21 years.

I wrote a lot of children's books that never got published. Maybe ten. I don't know how many times in my life I've had opportunities that I've been ill-prepared for. I remember one time sitting on a plane with all these great ideas in my head. I had been bumped up to first class and sitting next to me was a high-level executive of Random House Publishing. I don't know what his name was, it was about twenty years ago. He asked 'what do you do?' I said, 'I write children's books.' I told him one of my stories. He loved it and asked me to send it to him the next week. The problem was, I hadn't actually written the story. I had the idea and I scribbled stuff, but it wasn't on paper. So I wrote it and rewrote it and rewrote it, and I still wasn't happy. About three months later, I finally sent it off. Unfortunately, by that time, he had shifted positions and was gone. Now possibly, if I'd had that story on paper and could have shot it off to him the next day,

I might have been published much sooner. I wasn't prepared for the opportunity.

The first book I wrote that did get published was called *The Big Cheese* and I had sent it off time and time again, getting nothing but rejections. Probably about a hundred. I did not have an agent. I tried to do it myself. What happened was that I talked about my book. I started going to schools and reading it. Eventually I read it to a school and I got a call from someone who said 'hey my kid heard the story you read, can I buy it?' I replied to her that I didn't have it published yet and she volunteered 'I know a publisher, can I have him call you?' The guy phoned me and it was a local publisher in town. He published my first four books. And that was because I was sharing it, I was out there. It was a great experience.

Once I had my four books published by the small publisher, I decided I wanted to go for the big time.

It was a very interesting situation. Each week, I sent off ten query letters at a time to publishers. The next week I would send off another ten. I sent off a bunch one time and got a lot of rejections. I was overseas and I called my wife and asked her to send off the next ten. She made a mistake and sent them to ten publishers who had already rejected me. One of them was Free Spirit Publishing and they said they liked my work. Ironically, they wanted to publish my book after they had initially said no.

After two of my books had been published by Free Spirit Publishing, *How to Do Homework Without Throwing Up* and *Bullies are a Pain in the Brain*, I sent off a manuscript for a book I wrote called *Under the Big Sky*.

One day, I saw a receptionist at the front of a large publishing house chewing gum and sorting through the mail. As I watched, she was throwing some manuscripts on one pile and others on another. I asked her what was on the one pile and she said 'oh that stuff is not good.' I realized in amazement that this gum-chewing receptionist was the person determining whether a manuscript was good enough. I couldn't believe it. At that moment, I changed. I decided I will never take rejection personally again. It is only one person's interpretation of whether my writing is good enough or not, and I can't let that beat me down. I got really determined. That was an important growth point for me in terms of doing something for myself and not for anybody else. I write because the process is fantastic, and I share stories because they're great for other people to learn from. If somebody likes one, wonderful—if they don't, it doesn't mean that I'm a bad writer. It doesn't mean that the idea isn't good. It just means that one person doesn't care for that particular book.

The biggest thing that I had to overcome was fear of what people would think of my work, fear of being judged, fear of being told I was bad, fear of finding myself back in that special ed class where I was told I was an idiot. Fear of being judged and categorized as not successful. It was all about overcoming my fears. Being rejected made me even more determined.

Although I had just had my first books published, I was still fearful. There was a deciding point when I shifted from fear to determination. I am on the Board of the Childhood Cancer Foundation, the Candlelighters. One day I was at the hospital and someone had told me the story about a butterfly. It went like this: a man was sitting and reading his newspaper and saw a cocoon. Looking at it closely, he saw a little butterfly trying to get out. He watched this for about an hour. Eventually he felt bad for this little butterfly and wanted to help it. He got a pair of scissors, gently cut the cocoon open and carefully took the top off. Inside was the little butterfly all fragile looking and wet. He thought he'd done a great thing and saved it a lot of trouble. Well the next day, he came back and the butterfly was dead. Puzzled, he went to his school and said to his biology teacher: 'I don't know what happened, there was this beautiful butterfly and I cut open the cocoon to help it, and now it's dead.' The teacher replied, 'that's the problem, that butterfly needs to go through the pain and squeeze through that little hole. During the struggle of breaking though, all the fluid gets pushed into its wings so it can fly.' I realized that as people we need to experience that pain of growth, to be able to fill our wings and fly as well.

A few days later, I was at the hospital and there was a young girl whose name was Renee. She was five years old and had brain cancer. I was very close to Renee and her mom, and Renee called me her boyfriend. Renee was desperately ill, a bag of bones. Every day we would rock her, and one day the mother asked me to hold Renee while she took a shower. Renee was in a coma, very close to dying and I asked 'what happens if she dies while you're gone?' Renee's mother told me that she felt Renee was holding on for her sake even though she was in so much pain, and at this point she wanted her daughter to be free. While I held Renee, I whispered in her ear. Renee can you do me a favor? I want you to be a butterfly with big beautiful wings, because you are uncomfortable and you don't need to be here anymore. We will be okay. I want you to be a butterfly and fly away to where it's beautiful and free and you're not feeling uncomfortable anymore. Right after I said these words she took a big breath and died in my arms.

After that, I realized I'm not scared of going to places that I was scared of going to before. What am I really afraid of? I had been so afraid of judgment but how can someone else's judgment really hurt me? It can't. I hurt myself by my interpretation of their judgment.

Now I am so jazzed when I get rejected that I say, 'Oh man, you don't know what you're missing. I'm going to take this great work somewhere else.'

For a period of time, from the ages of 18 to 35, I worked in advertising because I couldn't see a way to start with my dream. I didn't see an outlet for writing children's books in South Africa and making any money doing it, and my next-door neighbor had an ad agency. All through my childhood he saw me writing, drawing and sketching, and he said 'you should be a copywriter.' He invited me to intern with his agency. I couldn't see a way to start with my dream, so I took an adjacent path. I liked copywriting in the beginning. I began as a copywriter and then graduated up the ranks until I became Creative Director for well-known agencies such as Saatchi and Saatchi, Ogilvy & Mather and Grey Advertising.

During my advertising years, I was still writing children's books and hiding them underneath my work. I actually got fired from an agency once. Stan Katz caught me doing this and said, 'Trevor why don't you write children's books instead of doing advertising. You're much better at writing children's books.' Although I had won 12 Clio awards—the highest honor in advertising—he fired me. It was just becoming evident that my true passion was writing children's books and not advertising.

Increasingly, I viewed my work as trying to convince people to buy things they didn't need. I loved it in terms of the brainstorming, the creativity and building teams, but eventually I hated the purposelessness of many of the projects I worked on. When I look back though, I realize that the skills I learned in my advertising career have helped me. I learned about giving presentations, I learned the art of the pitch. I learned how to market my books and myself. This is of great value to me now.

It's important to remember that you're never done. Even if you've made a shift in your life, you can get comfortable and may need to shift again.

My purpose has morphed and shifted. I started at age eight wanting to write and illustrate books, and I became published at age 35. Now I visit very sick children in hospitals and travel around the world doing public speaking. I never knew this would happen but it has become a major part of my career. I love it as much as I love writing because it fills the need I have to share my excitement. I wanted to share my excitement through books but someone needs to actually sit down and read them. By speaking, I can share the amazing experiences that have happened to me in a completely different way.

What people don't realize is that they have everyday experiences that are really magical and direct us to where we need to go, but a lot of people don't see the forest through the trees. They don't see the signs even though they are absolutely everywhere. Signs come in the strangest ways, in the strangest forms and I now know it's a sign because I'm open to it. I meditate after running every morning. I clear my mind. I think of it as a chalkboard... full of crap. And I get the eraser and I slowly erase everything so I can start my day totally clean. There are everyday experiences that direct us to where to go next. You just need to be open and receptive to them.

My words of wisdom to people trying to find their purpose is that once you have an inkling of what stirs you, really dig. Find out where that source of light is coming from. Ask yourself, how would I like someone else to value me? What would I like to leave as my legacy? Everyone's got a passion. Be relentless in trying to find what it is that's moving you."

9

THE DETERMINING FACTOR

Start by doing what's necessary; then do what's
possible; and suddenly you are doing the impossible.

—St. Francis of Assisi

The difference between knowing where you want to go, and actually getting there, is discipline. It *is* the determining factor. Discipline is how you will maintain complete and total focus, allowing you to overcome the obstacles that present themselves along the way.

Trevor's story is one of discipline. Discipline of the mind, body, soul and actions. He overcame the odds of a learning disability, staying determined even when the bullies were trying to beat him down. He kept himself in shape to have the energy and drive to do what he needed to do. He learned to get quiet and allow inspiration, trusting his own sense of what is good, choosing not to be derailed by others and overcoming fear.

DISCIPLINE OF THE MIND

Discipline of the mind means having confidence, strength and commitment—confidence in your ability to make it in life and knowing that you have enough inner strength and guidance to perform your chosen work. You believe in yourself. Life can be tough and challenges will be thrown your way, but you have an unshakable belief that you can handle it.

To improve your discipline, monitor your thoughts and incorporate the following practices to keep your mind sharply focused:

- *Break the chains of negative thought.* As soon as you recognize a limiting thought—fear, uncertainty, doubt, limitation, guilt—replace it with your vision and a positive affirmation. Even if the affirmation is something as simple as "I will make some small headway today." Remind yourself of the progress you've already made in the past week, month and/or year. It helps to write down your accomplishments so you can feel a real sense of satisfaction. Positive thoughts help diffuse resistance.

- *Rally against the fear and stop all self-effacing and tentative behaviors.* This means actively weeding out self-doubt. The first step is awareness. Notice when you are back-tracking on yourself, or giving yourself excuses of why your dream might not work out. Watch your language; it can create your reality. When starting my business, I would find myself saying "well if that doesn't work out, I can always go back to Corporate America." I was constantly thinking of sell-out plans and how I could rationalize them. I was putting my energy into all sorts of contingency plans instead of deliberately keeping the focus. When you are tempted to compromise and settle for something easier... don't. The more clear and more intentional you are, the faster you will create momentum.

- *Closely guard your confidence and sense of self-worth.* If you feel it slipping, remind yourself of how valuable you are and that your time is precious. If you have moments when you can't see this for yourself, seek out someone who will see it for you (a coach, co-worker, friend, family member). You can't pursue your Professional Destiny if you feel you don't deserve it or that you are unable to achieve it. Notice these thoughts as they surface—and then say goodbye to them. Replace them with renewed thoughts of your vision.

- *Keep a winning perspective.* You cannot achieve your Professional Destiny by seeing yourself as a victim. When life gets tough and things are challenging, choose to see yourself as an adventurer overcoming the odds rather than as a helpless victim.

- *Make commitments.* Every morning make two commitments: a "To Be" commitment based on who you want to be today and a "To Do" commitment based on what you want to achieve. Your "To Be" commitment sets the tone for the day. It is important to state it in the present tense, as if it's already happening. Examples: "Today I am productive," or "today I am insightful," or "today I am open and receptive to new ideas." After you set your "To Be" commitment, make a "To Do" list tied to the importance of your goals. Determine what step is necessary to make something happen. As you complete a task, cross it off your list. However small the task, this will give you a sense of satisfaction.

- *Value your time.* Another important part of discipline is not making appointments to see people when there is no higher purpose to seeing them. Your time is your most important asset. Value it.

- *Align your thoughts with the future you want to create.* Your thoughts are weaving your reality, so be aware of the reality your thoughts are creating. Are your thoughts from the past—or from your vision? Dwelling on thoughts from your past can hold you back, while thoughts of the future can begin creating a new reality. Are your thoughts serving you? If not, change them to align with your vision.

- *Enlarge your view of possibilities.* Look openly at things and see all possibility. Don't see only what your eyes see right in front of you. If you do, you accept limitation. Actively search to see new potential.

DISCIPLINE OF THE BODY

To accomplish anything great, you must make sure your mind and body are fit for the task. You must have the stamina, strength and essentials that you need—but *only* the things you need. You must leave all the extra weight behind.

Like a ship sailing at sea, outside forces will affect your journey, but you are the captain of your ship and you alone determine your course. If there's a storm raging and drama all around you, your inner guidance, or compass, will be drowned out and you will likely be tossed around. You must have your ship in good working order and your crew, or people who support you, in place.

- *Hone yourself for your best performance.* Like a true professional, you need to practice your gift every day. To do this you must be fit, rested and have your physical and mental capacities about you. Avoid substances that numb your mind and distract you from your goals. Focus on being alert and clear.

- *Get energized.* To pursue your passion, you must have energy and be strong enough to be in the places you need to be. Your body is what gets you there so it is important to take care of it. Healthy food is like high-performance fuel. Your engine will work better with it. You need energy to go the extra mile and accomplish your goals.

- *Get active.* Physical activity and exercise gets you revved up. During any physical training you develop good habits that serve you in life such as developing mental toughness to get through pain, becoming laser-focused and forcing yourself to continue even when you feel like quitting.

- *Do not see yourself as trapped inside a limited body.* Your greatest driver is your will—your will to succeed. With a strong will you can accomplish almost anything.

- *Be physically and mentally prepared for a race of learning and doing.* Prioritize your action items and plot your course. Meet your appointments. Jump over any hurdles that threaten to hold you back so you can put them behind you. And then go full speed.

- *Lose the weight.* This refers not so much to your physical weight, as your energetic weight. Streamline your relationships and your possessions and take only the essentials that you need. This means pulling the plug on draining or unhealthy relationships and breaking the bonds to unnecessary material possessions that keep you anchored. Take an honest, hard look at the people that you associate with. I call this "losing the weight." There are people who support you and help you to feel empowered, positive and on the right track. When you are with them you feel supported and energized. Then there are people who operate from a negative space, the naysayers, the ones who bring you down. You'll know them by the feeling you have when you are with them—you feel deflated, like the wind was just taken out of your sails. You feel drained when you are around them. Evaluate the people you spend time with and imagine yourself standing on a small platform. Then evaluate your friends, colleagues and even family members. Decide if they tend to lift you up to the next step with their ideas and positive energy, or drag you down off the platform with their pessimism and negativity. If they drag you down, limit your exposure to them and seek out people who inspire you. This may be difficult with family, but you can explain your purpose, hold firm to your commitment and ask them for their support even if they don't agree. Try to clearly identify the people who have your highest good in mind and surround yourself with them. Always try to put yourself in the highest, most supportive environment you can find.

DISCIPLINE OF THE SOUL

The majority of those who are successful in finding their purpose meditate and write down goals. They seek honesty about themselves and strive to be fully authentic. It takes discipline to hear your soul. Here are some ways that will help you tune in:

- *Get quiet.* Your inner voice is the voice that tells you whether something is true or false, right or wrong. You must get quiet and take time to hear it. To do this, dedicate time to allow your mind to become still. Start with fifteen minutes each day and within a few weeks move up to thirty minutes. This quiet time can be through meditation, drawing, painting, walking your dog in the early morning, or simply sitting silently in nature. The key is that this time must be peaceful and mind-less.

- *Go within.* Pause periodically and remind yourself about what you are really up to. Ask yourself how your daily activities are getting you closer to your vision. Try to make decisions that will get you closer to your greater goal. However, if you get stuck and feel that you can't do it yourself, ask for help—meditate, pray or find a friend who can inspire you and get you back on track. Realize that you have help and don't try to do it alone.

- *Become centered in the present.* It is a mistake to think that busy-ness in itself will provide you with the fastest route to success. Often it just distracts you from your goals. Pause for a few moments and become centered in the present. When you do, you expand your mind and will be able to work smarter and more creatively. You can actually get more done by doing less, and it will seem relatively effortless. By practicing the discipline of centering yourself in the present, you'll add powerful tools to your toolbox and be able to make the transformation from working hard to working smart.

- *Invite inspiration.* Your inner voice steers you and provides direction, but you must clear the clutter from your mind to hear it. Often it will come as a flash of inspiration. When you feel it, follow it.

- *Own your soul and make it unsellable.* Once you get in touch with your soul and know your dream, make it unsellable. Don't give in. Not for more money, not for more security, not to follow the path of least resistance.

DISCIPLINE OF ACTIONS

The famous Roman philosopher, Seneca, said in the mid-first century: "Luck is what happens when preparation meets opportunity." Trevor related in his story that at one of his first major opportunities (as an aspiring author sitting on an airplane next to the executive from Random House Publishing), he had an invitation to send his manuscript directly to an influential decision maker in the publishing world. This could have been quite lucky. As it turned out, he wasn't yet prepared and the opportunity passed by. It then took several more years and a great deal of hard work before his book got published. Perhaps he could have saved himself a lot of time and effort if he had taken a little time every day to transfer the book written in his head to become a book written on paper. The moral of this story is simply: always be prepared. If you are, you will be able to capitalize on the situation when a golden opportunity comes along.

These are effective ways to prepare for opportunities:

- *Prioritize.* Determine the things that need to be done in order to meet your goal and prioritize them in order of importance.

Make time to practice your gift every day, whatever it is, by reading, studying or building a network of people who can support your efforts, inspire you and help move you along.

- *Be decisive.* When you face a choice and need to make a decision, choose what means the most to you, even if it's difficult. Deciding is the first step. Even if you make a wrong decision, you are at least making movement and gaining experience. You can quickly correct it. Remember: not deciding *is* deciding. It is deciding to do nothing.

- *Take action.* Discipline of action and procrastination are polar opposites. Conquer the resistance that tends to want to put short-term gratification first. Get determined and weed out any urge to procrastinate as soon as you feel it take hold. Then walk your talk and have your actions match your commitments.

- *Handle the difficulties.* Life is tough, and having discipline means that you handle the difficulties. After all, problems do not go away by themselves. Ignoring your problems and unpleasant tasks is an act of procrastination. We hope our problems will go away, pretend they don't exist or skirt around them instead of facing them head-on. A natural tendency is to want to handle the more pleasant tasks at hand first, but that just keeps the problems looming out on the horizon, like a big, depressing weight pulling you down. It can affect your mood, your health and your sense of initiative. Difficult situations must be addressed head-on or remain a block to your growth, development and critical next step. They stand in the way of your full potential. Discipline is necessary to solve a problem and make headway. When you face a significant challenge, develop an action plan and write the steps down. Then force yourself to tackle part of it, or all of it, before you do anything else—especially the things that are easier. This is an act of self-discipline and its benefit is that you can put the unpleasant things behind you, have a sense of accomplishment and look forward to a more pleasant future.

- *Get determined.* Growth is a journey, and on any journey you will encounter unforeseen obstacles. Your ability to overcome these barriers will determine whether you succeed. It takes complete dedication, a whatever-it-takes mindset.

- *Practice, practice, practice.* Practice your gift every day and develop your skills. Be willing to be a student and take time to learn. People who become the best at what they do devote time to their chosen profession. Set aside a chunk of time every day. This is easy if you do what you love, and love what you do.

- *Be responsible.* Realize that you are the driver of your life and you have the ability to respond to each situation. Take ownership. You cannot take a hands-off approach and expect to become a master of your gift.

- *Dare to be remarkable.* If you pattern yourself after others, you will be like others and consequently will be... ordinary. The people who show an absolute conviction to make it, who pick themselves up when they fall, who fully invest their effort, time and energy, are the ones who accomplish extraordinary results.

10

SIGNS, LETTING GO & SYNCHRONOUS MOMENTS

Manifestation is an act of trust. It is the soul pouring
itself out into its world, like a fisherman casting
a net to gather in the fish he seeks; with each cast
properly made, we will bring what we need to us,
but first we must hurl ourselves into the depths
without knowing just what lies beneath us.

—David Spangler

So how do we find our way? Notice little shifts or recognize small things and pay attention to them. Take yourself out of your comfort zone and put yourself in a situation to find those changes. Open yourself to look for those pointers that will help you find your direction. Most people are expecting things to come to them without opening themselves up to receive them. For example, when Caroline Boudreaux felt dead in the water with the progress she was making with Indian adoptions, a friend pointed out that she should go back to India. Because she was openly seeking direction, she took a huge risk and used all of her savings to go. While there, she discovered her next steps. Nurture your intuition.

We often say, "I need to make money." And what do we do?

We go and look for a job; we network and look for postings online. But then we say, "I need to discover my purpose," and we are at a loss. We come to a halt. We need to open ourselves up to things we've never been open to before. When looking for our direction in life, we need to actively seek direction, be open to pointers and signs, and take a step forward with conviction. It's important to look within a scope that stimulates us. Many times finding our direction in life starts with volunteering because when we give of ourselves, new channels start opening. Things are in front of us every single day. We can choose to engage in something that drives us or we can say "I'm going to wait for it to come to me." We may also say, "I don't know what my direction is, but God will bring it to me"—but this doesn't work because we have to demonstrate our commitment first and seek out and take our next step, before we get help. When we do get direction, it can be very faint and we have to be open and receptive to notice. Other times it is stronger, like a hammer hitting you over the head. And even though you can't help but notice, you still have to be open to a different possibility than what you had originally planned for yourself.

For example, when I was leaving my full-time marketing position and going through a divorce, I became set on a "game plan" of moving to California with my daughter and being closer to family. Every night at dinner, I said the same prayer, "Please show me my path and make me receptive to it." Fortunately, I added the receptivity part because knowing myself, I thought I might be shown my path but not acknowledge it, because I was so set on what I wanted to do. That addition turned out to be essential.

After leaving the company, I told everyone I was moving to California. I put my house on the market, I began looking for jobs in California and I steadfastly refused to consider any position in Austin. It was 2001 and the dot.com boom had just gone bust. Austin, as much of the nation, was suffering. As soon as I put my house up for sale, the real estate market crashed. I interviewed for another executive-level job in California, but I couldn't get myself very excited. Finally, in my closing interview, the CEO told me I was perfectly qualified for the position, but I hadn't convinced him that I really wanted it. It was true—although I was quite disappointed that I couldn't fake it better. The next week, in the Whole Foods parking lot, I ran into the owner of the advertising agency that I worked with for a few years as a client. She asked me to lunch. During our meeting, she offered me a position at her firm, but I politely declined saying that I was moving. We had hit it off at lunch though, so we decided to meet again.

A month later, we had another lunch and this time she offered me a consulting role to help her grow her business. I realized that it was going to take longer than I expected for my house to sell, so I agreed to do it for two months until the end of the summer.

During those two months, I wrote a marketing plan for a large, Fortune 100 company which received funding for millions of dollars. I was ecstatic and thoroughly enjoying my work, but still intent on moving. Then another company unexpectedly offered me a lucrative commission to help them and the two efforts tied together seamlessly. At the time, though, my house still wasn't selling, I hadn't found a new job in California and during one of our walks, my daughter told me that she liked living in Austin with just the two of us.

Finally, during an appointment with my counselor, I related all of this. She made this wise observation: "Wait a minute. You mean to tell me that every night you pray for signs to show you the right path, and then your house doesn't sell, your daughter tells you she wants to stay, you get turned down for a job in California and you have a very profitable consulting business doing something that you love in Austin. How many signs do you need?"

To that I lamely replied, "Yes, but the signs aren't *right!*"

The signs might be there. They may hit you over the head, but you may still be blind to what's right in front of you, especially if you are set on another agenda. It's good to ask for openness and receptivity. And help—if you can't see it for yourself. Thankfully the truth prevailed in my case and my counselor helped me see it. For several years, I enjoyed pursuing the next, crucial part of my career in Austin.

STEP INTO THE FLOW

The Universe, or the source, is where creativity comes from. It is also where prosperity comes from. When you are in touch with the source, and the state of being, you step into the flow. You experience a sense of aliveness, energy and creativity. When you drop the fear, you also experience that you have enough. You may even become wildly prosperous because you are doing what you love and it is your gift.

The saying "go with the flow" is very wise. If we could learn to do it, our journey would be so much faster, easier and more enjoyable. We need to become flexible, adaptable and willing to let things morph and change as they will. Let go of being right. Attachment to our own point of view blinds us to greater opportunities. Get comfortable with uncertainty. When you are uncertain, you tend to be more open to new possibilities and it can turn into your period of greatest opportunity.

If we are to fully participate in the unfolding process of the universe, we need to let life flow through us instead of attempting to control it. Plotting, scheming, managing, sorting and organizing with the intention of making your destiny happen yourself, will strip away all joy and will be less effective. It squashes true creativity and replaces it with less productive busy-ness. Remind yourself that the universe can do it better than you can, so why not let it help you? Why slay this dragon alone?

If you are crystal clear about your vision and honest about your current reality, you don't have to figure out every detail. Things start happening of their own accord. They may seem like miracles or coincidences. It is help from the universe because you are clear in your intent.

Have you ever had the experience of being so anxious for a call that you impatiently wait by the phone, unable to focus on anything else? Instead of putting trust in the universe, knowing that you've done what you can, and that the call will either come at the right time or was not meant to be—you remain tense and anxious, and the phone does not ring. Then, when you finally give in and relax, the call (or a better one) finally comes. Or you are trying to grow your business and you have just sent a proposal to a potential new client. You check your email every few minutes and get anxious when there is no response. Finally, you refuse to be at the mercy of things you can't control and go out to do something productive with your time. You let it go for a while and don't even think about it. When you come back and log on—there it is.

Control and resistance separate you from the flow. When you

are anxious, you are disconnected. Non-resistance does not make you weak. In fact, non-resistance, combined with wisdom, gives you a calm strength that is both flexible and powerful.

How do you enter the state of flow? Recognize the force greater than yourself and actively seek to tap into it. Consciously do things to feed your soul. Notice what you enjoy doing and what you are good at. Make some time to do these things and rekindle your creativity. Take trips. Take time to reflect.

The flow state is an altered state of consciousness we achieve when we are so engaged in an activity that nothing else matters. It is total focus. We experience the flow state in many ways: listening to music, writing, biking, meditating, praying, hiking, doing the work we love. In this state there is an extraordinary clarity, focus and concentration. Any effort we make feels more like play. We feel strong, alert, effortlessly effective and satisfied. We are at the peak of our ability and we experience an exhilarating feeling of transcendence. We become unaware of time.

Concentration, or being in the flow, means total absorption. We can only be masters of something that interests us greatly. Great leaders and great inventors are not bored with their work. If you pay attention, you will notice that you are experiencing moments of joy when you are creating, working and learning. You forget about the world around you and lose track of your surroundings, fully experiencing the joy of what you are doing.

You come into flow in your life when you awaken your sense of destiny. You fall out of flow when you renege on your gifts and potential, or when you ignore your deepest calling and settle for mediocrity. Our tasks cannot be too simple for our abilities or we become bored and less creative. Whether things are "seamlessly clicking" or "rapidly combusting" is a sign of whether you are in or out of step with the universe. When you are in step with the universe, things begin to fall into place. There is a high cost of getting out of synchronicity with the universe. You are on your own. You don't have help outside yourself. Nothing works out and you can't get a break. Things seem to spiral downwards and everything becomes a constant struggle. On the other hand, simplicity is a sign of being in the flow. Usually if something is simple, elegantly efficient and practically effortless, it is a wonderful indicator that you are on the right track.

WE GET HELP JUST AS WE NEED IT

Our guidance toward our purpose comes from within. You can't find it outside of yourself and you can't reach it by trying to build consensus. However, you are not expected to go it alone. You get help from the universe as you need it. Experienced people will show up along the way to help guide you.

We are in this state of being (flow) when we are receptive to life and all its possibilities, and when we are willing to take the next step as it is presented to us. When we do this, we meet the most remarkable people just as we need them, who help us with exactly what we are looking for. Miracles happen.

I've come to realize that the term "Godsend" is a perfect word. It means exactly what is says—someone or something sent from God (or the Universe) to help you just as you need it.

Upon returning from my second writing retreat and finishing the first draft of my book and proposal, I said to myself: "Now what? What's the next step? How do I format my proposal? What is it supposed to look like? What on earth are you supposed to bind it in?" Truly, I didn't have much of a clue. I knew how to write the content, but I didn't know the trimmings or the exact submission protocol. And being from a marketing background, I knew this was important. The person who had been around to guide me was unavailable for several weeks and I was feeling at a loss for the next step. I couldn't believe I was in this situation after working so enthusiastically and diligently for so long.

As I was driving home from a consulting meeting in the morning, I was thinking that I needed to answer an email from the marketing manager at the Miracle Foundation about the meeting I was to lead that evening. As I realized this, I noticed that I was about to pass the organization, so I thought "why don't you just quickly stop in instead of emailing? It would be nice to see everyone anyway." So I did. I went in to say hello and Caroline was in the middle of a meeting with someone who happened to be an author. She immediately introduced us. As we talked, I realized that this person had gone through the writing process of being a new author almost exactly as I did. Except she now had several books published. I couldn't believe my luck! She answered every one of my questions and promised to send me the proposal for her book that had been successfully published. This was perfect. I could see the format I was looking for and I knew precisely what I had to do. It was exactly the help I needed, at exactly the right time.

The part of this that continuously surprises me is how the help we need so often comes from an unexpected source. I have come to learn, though, that however this process happens... it works!

So don't try to do it alone, without help from the Universe or others. If you do, you are swimming against the current and it's difficult. There is help available, you just need to be open, go with your hunches and then be exceptionally grateful when it comes.

II

OBSTACLES & TESTS
(WHAT YOU NEED TO OVERCOME)

Pilgrim in your journey
you may travel far,
for pilgrim it's a long way
to find out who you are…

—Enya, *Pilgrim*

D o not expect the road to be short. It never is. You can have the destination in mind, but the journey will take you in directions you never imagined going before. Looking back you will see that these were places you needed to go. They were experiences you needed to have or lessons you needed to master to prepare you for your destiny—the job you are meant to do.

FEAR

What would you do if you weren't afraid?

—Spencer Johnson, *Who Moved My Cheese?*

In any undertaking of substance, we cannot expect ourselves to be fearless—we all have fear. The secret is to be courageous and not let our fear win over. Having courage is not the absence of fear but the drive and the strength to keep going in spite of it. Our desire and our vision must always be larger than our fear.

All human behaviors are motivated at their deepest level by one of two emotions—fear or love.

Fear is the energy that shrivels, contracts, depresses, shuts down, panics, flees, hoards, attacks, harms and destroys.

Love is the energy that expands, opens up, energizes, enjoys, shares, nurtures, heals, brings peace and creates.

You will notice this if you pay attention to the emotion behind the emotion, or the thought behind the thought. For example, being angry at your boss for not being selected to participate in a plum, high-profile project represents a fear of failure, or not being good enough.

Since we were young, we have been taught to live in fear. Fear of "not enough" and survival of the fittest.

Nothing stands between us and our highest purpose and the true desire of our heart, as much as doubt and fear. FEAR is an acronym for False Evidence Appearing Real. It is our greatest enemy. Most often the fear of suffering is worse than the suffering itself. Fear of failure, fear of scarcity or "not enough," fear of sickness, fear of loss, fear of humiliation—all stop us from moving forward. We must substitute faith for fear. If you think about it, fear is really faith in the negative. It is faith in failure instead of faith in success.

Years ago, early in my marketing career, my peers and I used to pride ourselves in spreading FUD—fear, uncertainty and doubt—about our competition. We looked at it as a fundamental business game and took great relish in mastering it. FUD also stands in the way of achieving your purpose, and your mind is a master at it. It is the single greatest obstacle to accomplishing your purpose because it is insidious and can show up at every step of the way. The larger your purpose, the larger your fear, uncertainty and doubt will present itself. Expect this. Anytime you do something big, you can expect big challenges. They go hand in hand. Some fear is good, it can keep you safe, but the majority of fear only holds you back. Once you take a stand and commit to your vision, the fear that weighs you down will dissipate and you will make faster progress toward your goal. Anytime you experience new fear, it is a sign that you need to re-commit to your vision and re-commit to action. Make forward movement and the fear will take care of itself.

The question to ask yourself is, "what would you do if you weren't afraid?"

EISENHOWER AND D-DAY

As the pressure mounts and strain increases,
everyone begins to show the weaknesses in his makeup.
It is up to the Commander to conceal his;
above all to conceal doubt, fear and distrust.

—General Dwight D. Eisenhower

In December of 1943, General Dwight D. Eisenhower was selected to become the Supreme Commander of the Allied Expeditionary Force and lead the D-Day military invasion against the Nazi forces in World War II. D-Day was the largest amphibious military invasion in history and the single most important operation to determine the outcome of the war. The target date was June 5th, 1944 and preparations had been begun more than a year before. By the end of May, over two million men, 5,000 ships and thousands of bombers were stationed in Britain. Eisenhower oversaw it all.

As Supreme Commander, Eisenhower's responsibilities included reporting to an American president, an English Prime Minister and providing leadership and direction to six chiefs of staff. Ultimately, it was up to Eisenhower to decide how to land nine divisions of sea and airborne troops on a 50-mile stretch of hostile shores within 24 hours. He had to give direction to over 150,000 men, keep the invasion site location secret from the Nazis, take in all the intelligence gathered from a network of sources, make sense out of it and decide what to do. It was up to him to weigh the risks and make the best decision possible given the information he had at the time. He faced enormous pressure every day, yet he couldn't abdicate—he had to take the responsibility and act. The success or failure of the operation, thousands of men's lives and the outcome of the war rode on his decisions. His job was a lonely one and he carried an awesome burden of command.

On the last few days leading up to D-Day when everything was meticulously planned, Eisenhower's strength, courage and resolve were severely tested when a storm arose in the English Channel that threatened the success of the entire operation.

For two days, Eisenhower had to choose whether to risk the hazardous weather conditions and poor visibility, or postpone invasion and risk the secrecy of the operation. The course of the war and men's lives depended on his decision and the solution was far from evident. It all came down to the wire. The air, navy and land forces were poised to go, yet due to dense low cloud, heavy rain and hazardous conditions, Eisenhower made the agonizing choice to postpone for 24 hours. Finally, he received news of a slight, temporary break in conditions and had thirty minutes to decide whether to launch. If he decided against it, the tidal conditions would change for the worse and he would lose a window of opportunity for another two weeks.

The pressure was enormous and either choice was risky, but he faced his fears and made the best decision he could with the information he had. Looking out the window at the wind-driven rain, it didn't seem possible that the operation could go ahead but he weighed the alternatives and spoke the fateful words, "Okay, let's go."

During these incredibly tense days, his chief of staff mentioned that he was struck by the "loneliness and isolation of a commander at a time when such a momentous decision was to be taken by him, with full knowledge that failure or success rests on his individual decision."

Yet as with all great leaders, underneath his broad smile and easy manner, Eisenhower had an iron will and immense self-discipline. He had learned from his previous combat experience directing the Allied invasion forces in North Africa and Italy how critical it was for him to be optimistic in the presence of his subordinates and how costly caution can often be in combat. In fact, David Stafford writes in his book, *Ten Days to D-Day,* that Eisenhower was known to putt an imaginary golf ball around his office to relieve his extreme stress and appear calm to his visitors.

Of course Eisenhower had fear, but his vision to win the war was greater. As he said to his troops:

"This operation is not being planned with any alternatives. This operation is planned as a victory, and that's the way it's going to be. We're going down there, and we're throwing everything we have into it, and we're going to make it a success."

They did... and as a result, changed the course of the war. In a single day over 150,000 American, British, Canadian and French troops entered the coast of Normandy. The largest air, land and sea operation in history was a success, and victory in Europe became suddenly within reach. Because of a monumental act of courage by Eisenhower and so many other men, World War II, the Nazi regime and the massacre of millions of Jews and political prisoners ended a year later.

Looking back with 20/20 vision through history and knowing the outcome of D-Day and the war, it is hard to fully grasp the incredible fear, uncertainty and doubt that Eisenhower faced with each of his decisions. He had first-hand experience of the risks of making amphibious landings on hostile shores with the real possibility of sending thousands of men into useless slaughter if the Germans were prepared. Yet he used his best judgment, kept the grander, overall vision first and foremost in his mind and made the soul-racking decisions when he needed to.

Fears come in all different forms and on all different levels. There are wartime fears that Eisenhower faced—fear of survival, fear of loss, fear of failure—on the grand scale involving nations and thousands of men. And there are the exact same fears that we face on the personal level, perhaps involving only ourselves, when we venture into the unknown.

It is a given that you will have fear. It can feel paralyzing, but keep moving forward. Winston Churchill once said "If you're going through hell, keep going." Keep putting one foot in front of the other. The more you step up the pace, the faster you'll get out. It takes courage and a whole lot of faith, but ultimately if you want to get to reach a better place, you don't have much of a choice. So when you find yourself in a situation when you are suffering, fearful and in pain... keep going... take action... stay focused on the outcome you want so you can keep moving forward... and get out as fast as you can.

Finding and living our purpose isn't easy, and sometimes we just don't want to deal with what is facing us. It seems too big. Or, we believe we will face a hard time in the unknown, so we just tune everything out and hope things will get better. The unknown is uncomfortable and no matter how unfulfilled we are feeling in our current situation, we'd rather stay in a situation we know instead of venture out.

There is a great fear in moving from our familiar life, even if it is unsatisfying. We get to the point where we know "this is what I am not," but we don't yet know what we "are." We say to ourselves, "This is what I don't want, but I don't really know what I do want." In other words, we know our current situation isn't working for us, but we don't know what our new situation will be or what it will look like. We are "in between" and for most of us it's a very uncomfortable place to be. Shari Wynne, my dear friend and confidante, told me when I left my job as president of the advertising agency and was suffering with uncertainty:

"You know what the 'no' is, you just don't know what the 'yes' is. Don't try to frame the 'no,' don't focus on it. Listen for what's right. You're not the socialite you used to be. You don't care about social status. You're in the mixing place and in the middle of a paradigm shift. Just get used to it. Your former livelihood was kindergarten compared to now, this is college. It may not be pretty, it's just a matter of adjustment and a leap of faith that you'll get to the next level. At least you're asking the right questions."

GET COMFORTABLE WITH UNCERTAINTY

One doesn't discover new lands without consenting
to lose sight of the shore for a very long time.

—Andre Gide

Get comfortable with uncertainty—it's the time of our greatest opportunity. A time when all possibilities are open to us. If we hold our vision and resolve to take a step toward it each day, we can be assured that great uncertainty only lasts for a while. This too shall pass.

Oftentimes even when we start our journey, our fear of failing returns and our hope of finding our purpose fades. We have no proof that things will turn out the way we want so we are hesitant, or even unwilling, to take the risk. Sometimes it takes a great deal of pain to get us motivated. Our fearful beliefs immobilize us and slowly but surely kill our spirit. We can feel ourselves being drawn back to the comfort of familiar territory—even though we haven't been happy there for a long time. We become more anxious and wonder if we are crazy for wanting to do this.

Sometimes fear can be good. It can motivate us into action,

especially if we fear our situation will get worse if we don't act now. But it is not good when it paralyzes us from moving forward. This is the point when we look into the unknown, feel our fear, take a deep breath and step forward anyway. Do it even if you're scared.

If you are willing to do the thing you are afraid to do, you often do not have to. Face the situation fearlessly and watch it dissipate.

Most things we worry about never actually happen. So worrying is an unproductive emotion that drains our energy and creative forces. Sometimes we just need to find humor in our fears.

It's like setting sail. We do not like the idea of having to set out into open seas because it seems dangerous and we have no idea if we will get lost. But we have to catch ourselves and laugh when we think like this, because the alternative is to stay anchored at the dock forever, or just sail in the same comfortable, but boring patterns within the harbor.

The longer you stay in an unfulfilling and unchallenging situation, the more resigned you become—and the more you risk losing your individuality, unique gifts and edge.

COMFORT AND COMPLACENCY

A ship in harbour is safe,
but that is not what ships are built for.

—William Shed

Complacency, fear of change, comfort. Those are the factors that mask your true direction and your true passion.

Let's say you come up with a vision for yourself that you'd like to venture out on your own and start a business. Immediately the fear kicks in that you will have to sacrifice, you might not be able to afford all the things you are used to, you might have to move into unknown territory, you might have to struggle and, worst of all, you don't know what's out there. Your mind tells you maybe it's better to stay right where you are in the known and comfortable. Abandoning your vision seems like the safer, most logical choice.

During the last six months of my earlier role at the advertising agency, I became increasingly disenchanted and I knew I had to make a change. I was struggling more every day and was praying for guidance and the courage to do what I needed to do next. I received multiple signs that clearly indicated that it was time to move. The first was a story called "Stepping Off the Cloud," which came to me at a perfect time.

STEPPING OFF THE CLOUD

A friend of mine heard a story at church; it went something like this:

A woman was standing on a cloud. The cloud represented a bad situation. She desperately wanted to get off, but couldn't find any way to get down without stepping into thin air. She paced back and forth, searched the cloud up and down, looking for any possible way. There was none. Things were getting worse and she knew she had to jump, but was too afraid. So she tried something else. She spent weeks and months laying down as many safety nets as possible to catch her when she fell. Finally, she reached the point of no return and couldn't bear it any longer. She didn't know if any of her safety nets would hold, but she jumped anyway.

For a split-second after she took that first critical step, she stood completely off the cloud in mid-air. Then quietly and gently, from out of nowhere, God's hand appeared under her feet and carried her softly down.

The reason my friend told me this story was that I was in an increasingly painful situation in my career. I needed out. I knew I had to leave, but I didn't know yet where I was going to land. I had a daughter in a very expensive university and another in high school, on her way to a very expensive university and I was the primary provider. I did have some savings but it wouldn't be enough to retire, and I was beside myself with anxiety. As my work situation grew worse and worse, I started having physical symptoms. My stomach started to churn, my face was starting to feel numb, I lost my appetite (this never happens!) and I could only force down the blandest of bland food. I lost eight pounds in one month without trying and finally, my heart began to race. I was definitely in survival, fight-or-flight mode. It wasn't pretty. I wanted to be "let go" to get certain terms in my employment contract, but that didn't seem to be happening. I was laying down safety net after safety net of consulting opportunities and job interviews, but it was still early on and I didn't feel "set." I tried bargaining with the Universe—but unfortunately it wasn't buying my proposals of how my best-laid plans should work.

In the middle of this period of job transition agony, I looked for signs to help point me in the right direction. A few days after I heard the "Stepping Off the Cloud" story, I read an article in a magazine right before I went to bed. It was about a woman who had separated from her husband but could not seem to make the final break. Here is an excerpt:

> "…during an Outward Bound expedition in Maine, the one exercise that had paralyzed me involved standing on a rope stretched tight between two poles, high above the ground. Wobbling uncontrollably, I had found it impossible to let go of the overhead knot I was grasping for balance in order to lunge for the next overhead knot, dangling just out of reach. I couldn't go back and I couldn't move forward. I came to think of it as a metaphor for the anxiety I felt for leaving the safety of the past for the uncertainty of the future."
> —Susan Tifft, *More Magazine,* October 2005

As I read this, it struck me as the perfect metaphor for the situation I was in. I didn't want to let go of my current position, salary and stature, yet I was empty, suffering and couldn't eat. I wanted to move forward, but couldn't bring myself to let go first. I called my good friend the next day and read the passage to him. He agreed that this story represented my situation to a tee. Like Outward Bound and the Woman on the Cloud, I needed to let go in order to move forward.

One day later, out of the blue, I received an email in my inbox. The subject line jumped out at me—it literally said:

"Let Go and Live!"

It was a message forwarded to me from Katie Laine, my executive coach, who had not heard the story, or known I had read the magazine article. I knew enough to know that this was more than a coincidence. It was a sign, clear as day.

Here's what the email said:

> "'Let go and live. The greatest danger to life is to try to secure it. In order to hold God's hands and really live, we have to let go of things like comfort and big plans.'
> —M. Craig Barnes

> For the so many out there who are making big plans that make sense to the mind and are comfortable to the ego, thinking that this is the key to making good things possible, I say 'Think again!' The 'shock-and-awe' approach to life—jumping off the cliff... risking everything, completely, with no holds barred, for that *one* thing you must do, that you were literally made to do here—is the only one that delivers the goods."

I couldn't believe it said "jumping off a cliff." I had just heard that the day before in the "Stepping Off the Cloud" story. It was a direct and unmistakable sign.

I was getting signs like this almost every day—messages through my friends, articles I read, songs and chance meetings with wise individuals, just as I needed them. I knew I had to make a change—it was inevitable—but it was still incredibly hard to do.

I came back from my life-changing trip to India and decided to hand in my resignation, no matter what the outcome would be. If the orphans I visited could thrive so beautifully without a future planned out for them, so could I. I had finally surrendered and reached the point of no return. I knew I couldn't do another day. I gave my notice and started my new adventure.

Once you become inclined to discover and embark upon your life's purpose, and gain the strength to overcome inertia, the next level of your journey begins. We alternate between the exhilaration of fully living life, and fear and anxiety of facing the unknown.

Part of us wrestles with fearfulness and the denial of our ability to make a real difference in the world. We may go through the "why me" syndrome and think that if we stand real still, fade into the background and become invisible, someone else will get picked and we'll thankfully get passed over, so we can return to our comfort zone. Other times, moments of rationality will take over and say "Have you lost your mind, are you nuts? I can't do this. So and so will do this, it's more suited for her anyway." Then we thank God for a moment of rationality again. But, unless we bury our heads in the sand, or keep ourselves so occupied that we can't reflect, the call comes back.

I kept denying my destiny because of my insecurity, my fear of hurting my career and my lack of courage. I knew deep down that cooperating with my destiny would bring great responsibility as well as change and unfamiliarity. I was afraid of it. All I could think of was that I would have to become like Mother Teresa and serve others in poverty. As much as I admire her, I didn't think this was what I was meant to do. Knowing my direction and making a choice seemed overwhelming, so I resisted.

This is a huge burden to overcome. Our responsibility is to

take the first step and realize that we will get help. Once we take action, the universe will help us although it may continue to test our resolve. In the early days of the Miracle Foundation, Caroline Boudreaux got from unexpected sources exactly the amount of money she needed to keep her going forward. These "coincidences" are the universe in action.

In some ways we can't get past the fear of the unknown and the material sacrifice that we've convinced ourselves we'll have to make. We get fixed in our nest of security. Yet on the other hand, we can't quiet the persistent inner voice that points us in this new direction. If we observe ourselves carefully, we notice the thoughts, interests and actions that energize us are all directed toward this theme.

When I finally reached the moment of decision to resign, it was as if I had no real choice. It was not so much a decision about what I should do, it reached the point that I really couldn't do anything else. The moment I walked away, a strange thing happened. I had no idea how I would proceed, yet oddly enough, most of my concerns and doubts about the enormity of the situation were erased, and I had an incredible sense of freedom that I hadn't felt in a long time. I moved forward toward my destiny the moment my words became action.

The first test is stepping off the cloud. Once you do this, the universe opens up and you'll experience abundance and a sense of aliveness that you haven't experienced for far too long. A friend of mine told me, "Enjoy this time—it's magical—the universe is working with you. Go with it, don't kill it. The moment you reach back for 'safety' will be the moment it all stops." If you allow yourself to fall back into complacency to avoid the risk that comes hand in hand with fully living life, you may wake up to find one day that you are trapped there and can't get out.

Take one day at a time, one step at a time. Stay open and receptive, and most of all—enjoy.

COUNTER INTENTIONS

Sometimes we set an intention to grow our business, get published, win a race, find the love of our life... and it doesn't happen. What could be the cause? What is keeping us from our goal? Assuming we are in alignment with our purpose, it could be a counter intention. A counter intention is an intention we hold in our subconscious that holds us back. Most of the time we are not even aware of it. One way to find out if we are at the mercy of a counter intention is to honestly look at the outcomes that are happening in our life. In other words, if our intentions are X and our outcomes are Y we need to identify the counter intention that is causing Y instead of X. Then we need to bring it into the light, acknowledge it and decide if we want to continue holding that belief.

For example, after my divorce and a subsequent on-and-off relationship, I realized that I hadn't been seriously dating for over a year even though I had set an intention to find someone special to bring into my life. Thinking of counter intentions, I decided to try practicing what I preach and spent the morning meditating on what could possibly be holding me back. I said I wanted someone to love, but the outcome I was experiencing was clearly otherwise.

A few days later, I was sitting peacefully in my favorite chair thinking about dating and how quiet my house would be when my daughter went off to college and this thought passed through my mind: "I don't want an intruder in my life until Allie goes off to college." It floated by so quickly that it almost didn't register. Then the alarms started to sound and I realized, "you just called this new love you are looking for an *intruder!*"

I thought about it and realized this was my counter intention. Upon further reflection, I realized that I thought of a man as an intruder in many ways and I asked myself "well then should I wait until Allie goes off to school, or can I accept the view of this person as a welcome companion instead of an intruder?" I decided that as long as the relationship was calm and respectful of my time, I was ready to meet someone. Interestingly, I did meet someone who was non-intrusive and was with him until exactly the day Allie went off to school.

LIMITATION AND HABIT

Another obstacle to realizing your purpose is an ingrained sense of limitation that we place upon ourselves. We may have had a legitimate experience that taught us this, but it is something that we must shed. Limitation often comes out of habit and patterns of behavior that we have learned. For example, my dog is contained in the front and back yards by an invisible fence. As a puppy she was trained that if she crossed that boundary, she would receive a shock from her collar. Once she learned this, you could take her collar off and she would still stay within her boundary in the yard. She's a large, strong, German Shepherd mix and would still not venture out.

As people, we have been trained with our own sense of limitation. If we have taken a risk in the past and gotten "shocked," we are hesitant to take a risk again whether the perceived boundary is there or not. We have been trained that the limitation is real even if it now only resides in our mind and it can keep us from taking action. Trevor Romain was told as a child that he did not have enough talent to draw and this perception kept him from drawing for 21 years. Once he rid himself of this limitation in his mind, he began illustrating again and his work became published in thirty books and animated in videotapes.

12

FEARLESS FAITH

What exactly does it take to live the life of your dreams?
Perfect timing? Fortunate opportunities?
A million dollars in the bank? Not even close.
It takes a decision; A simple decision
that will ultimately test the strength of your
commitment and the depth of your faith.

—Karen Wright, *The Sequoia Seed*

Fear shows itself all along our journey. The more important our purpose is and the more remarkable we are called to be, the more we can expect to encounter fear. Anyone who is remarkable has overcome great difficulty and fear. If this weren't the case there would be more remarkable people—those who stand out as truly extraordinary. Most people choose to be ordinary. They play it safe and do just enough to get by.

What separates the extraordinary from the ordinary are those people who choose faith over fear and practice discipline every day in achieving their purpose. Faith, in this sense, means a passionate, unbending belief in your vision. Here are some things to know about faith:

- *Faith is believing in success.* It's believing in a friendly creative force bigger than yourself, a force that will help you. Fear is inverted faith—it is believing in failure.

- *Faith looks forward.* It is believing in your vision even when there's no proof. You may not know all the answers, but you know you will take the next step.

- *Faith is the tool to overcome fear.* Truly remarkable people call on it every day and guide their lives with it.

- *With faith, you don't get to know how it gets done.* You don't get to know what is going to happen either. "How" or "what" are not the questions—you just need to know that you are going to do it.

- *Faith and commitment get you there.* If you falter on either, the journey will take longer.

Expect that the process of moving along your path will throw challenges at you. It's part of the package. It's the hand you are dealt. When you think of it this way, you won't get mired in pessimism or misery. Or if you feel it, which is natural, you won't stay there for long. You know it's just something you need to get through. And you will.

Dr. Martin Luther King, Jr. spoke from experience when he said, "Take the first step in faith. You don't have to see the whole staircase. Just take the first step."

Focus on your vision but surrender the outcome. This is the wisdom of insecurity. Your job is to take the journey one step at a time—even if it is unsettling, even when you don't see where it is all leading. Accept what the universe does. If you do this, things will come naturally and you will know the next step. The outcome will take care of itself. So remember:

Take a leap of faith
Trust the journey
Surrender the outcome to the universe

If you feel blind and you can't see where it is all leading—let go. Know that the universe can see everything and will guide you. And understand that things in your life may at times seem to break down. If you want change and forward movement, some things must break. They must make room for the next better thing. If you keep moving, eventually you will get to where you want to be—or somewhere better. Have faith that even though you may not see it at the time, you will be able to see the perfection later.

Do not try to be too strategic by thinking, plotting and planning with your own essence. Rigidly defining things is limiting and security can be illusory. When you don't have to cling to things that bring you guarantees, you can participate more with what's directly in front of you. You decide to show up and experience what is happening instead of thinking what will happen. Trying to plot, sort and organize it all—trying to exactly define it—kills the joy and strips away the magic.

Have you ever noticed that some of the best things in life (career, relationships and unique opportunities) often come from out of the blue, unexpectedly? Usually they are not things we plan, specifically ask for, or even knew were a possibility. Instead they show up as a wonderful surprise... a business idea comes from someone we haven't talked to in years, a special person sits next to us at a coffee shop or on a plane, or an unexpected email shows up right in time to solve a problem just when we need it. The universe knows what we need better than we do. And it knows the best form to deliver it in.

Sometimes it's hard to have faith, when nothing seems to be happening, when things are going wrong or when you feel uncertain. Remember, fields lay fallow between seasons of growth. This is necessary to clear an opening, regroup, rest up and recharge. Between the growth seasons are seasons of formation. This is your time of formation.

When you are in sync with the universe, you are in the abundant flow of life and what you need comes to you when you need it. Have faith that right now you have enough. Assume you can accomplish whatever you set out to do. If you don't know how, it's okay, help will come to you. You have what it takes right now. There is no need to hold back and wait.

Set your vision of what you want, do your best, then relax and receive. Problems tend to resolve themselves and you will know your next step. Life will evolve you. You will have help as you need it, and you'll learn and grow naturally. Once you have faith in the process, you'll begin to enjoy yourself along the way.

The universe provides things for us that we cannot provide for ourselves. When we're in step with it, great things happen.

Go within and listen. Allow inspiration. The answer you seek may be a thought, a feeling or an event that solves the problem. Each morning, start by asking the universe to direct you and provide the people and circumstances that will make your day productive and fulfilling. Make this a co-creative process—you do your part by asking for what you need, becoming quiet and allowing yourself to sync up with the power of the highest creative force. The universe will do its part and provide the guidance you need—as well as the magic. Then remember to recognize the help you are getting and be grateful for it.

The way this works is like one big connect-the-dots puzzle. We may not immediately see how the individual dots connect, but the perfection is revealed later.

Steve Jobs illustrates this concept in his own "connect the dots" story:

"I dropped out of Reed College after the first six months, but then stayed around as a drop-in for another 18 months or so before I really quit. So why did I drop out? I naively chose a college that was almost as expensive as Stanford, and all of my working-class parents' savings were being spent on my college tuition. After six months, I couldn't see the value in it. I had no idea what I wanted to do with my life and no idea how college was going to help me figure it out. And here I was spending all of the money my parents had saved their entire life. So I decided to drop out and trust that it would all work out okay. It was pretty scary at the time, but looking back it was one of the best decisions I ever made. The minute I dropped out I could stop taking the required classes that didn't interest me, and begin dropping in on the ones that looked interesting.

It wasn't all romantic. I didn't have a dorm room, so I slept on the floor in friends' rooms, I returned coke bottles for the 5¢ deposits to buy food with, and I would walk the seven miles across town every Sunday night to get one good meal a week at the Hare Krishna temple. I loved it. And much of what I stumbled into by following my curiosity and intuition turned out to be priceless later on. Let me give you one example:

Reed College at that time offered perhaps the best calligraphy instruction in the country. Throughout the campus every poster, every label on every drawer, was beautifully hand calligraphed. Because I had dropped out and didn't have to take the normal classes, I decided to take a calligraphy class to learn how to do this. I learned about serif and sans serif typefaces, about varying the amount of space between different letter combinations, about what makes great typography great. It was beautiful, historical, artistically subtle in a way that science can't capture, and I found it fascinating.

None of this had even a hope of any practical application in my life. But ten years later, when we were designing the first Macintosh computer, it all came back to me. And we designed it all into the Mac. It was the first computer with beautiful typography. If I had never dropped in on that single course in college, the Mac would have never had multiple typefaces or proportionally spaced fonts. You can't connect the dots looking forward; you can only connect them looking backwards. So you have to trust that the dots will somehow connect in your future. You have to trust in something —your gut, destiny, life, karma, whatever. This approach has never let me down, and it has made all the difference in my life.

Stay determined, keep believing and stay committed."

UNANSWERED PRAYERS

Remember the saying "thank God for unanswered prayers"? Many people are in ignorance of their true destinies and are striving for things that ultimately would lead them down the wrong path bringing dissatisfaction and failure if they were attained. There is a profound difference between wanting and needing.

Fortunately, most often when you genuinely ask the Universe for your purpose to manifest, you are protected from getting things you want that are not on your path. You may think that your happiness depends on getting that particular thing at the time, but later you "thank God" that you didn't get it or you see the reason you were given something else.

Sometimes the direction we think we should head, or the things we think we need, are really not what we need at all. We need to have a constant openness and faith in the wisdom and guidance of a greater power.

The following poem full of Sufi wisdom clearly reflects the difference between our true needs and our wants:

> I asked for strength and God gave me difficulties to
>   make me strong
> I asked for wisdom and God gave me problems to
>   learn to solve
> I asked for prosperity and God gave me a brain and
>   brawn to work
> I asked for courage and God gave me dangers to
>   overcome
> I asked for love and God gave me people to help
> I asked for favours and God gave me opportunities
> I received nothing I wanted
> I received everything I needed.
>
> —Sufi poem, attributed to Hazrat Inayat Khan

Sometimes, painful as it is, being cast out is a favor to help you realize your destiny. Al Gore, the international spokesperson for global warming, barely and controversially lost his campaign for the presidency of the United States. This loss caused him to turn back to his passion as a spokesperson for the environment and bring worldwide awareness for a massive, global problem.

If Gore is right and we are systematically destroying our environment, then arguably there can be no greater cause for the world's population to address. Is it his highest calling to initiate awareness and change? Was his lost presidential campaign actually a failure (and if so, is it a failure similar to Steve Jobs being ousted from Apple in the early years?), or was it vitally directional toward his ultimate purpose? We can't fully know what setbacks, trials and tribulations mean at the time they occur and how they relate to ultimate purpose. Like Steve Jobs said: "You can't connect the dots looking forward; you can only connect them looking backwards" Time ultimately reveals the truth.

MORPH AND CHANGE

Change is constant. Flow with change and learn to thrive on it. Be flexible. Having discipline and a clear sense of purpose will allow you to be flexible and adaptable rather than rigid, while staying your course. The strongest trees are the ones that can bend instead of snapping apart in a fierce wind. Once you realize that you are not the sole person driving the ship—you have help—your life will become easier. Your purpose will morph and change. Let it morph, it needs to be malleable. Trust that you will know when you are off course.

Change is unavoidable. Reluctance to adapt to change will only keep you stuck. Growth demands the willingness to temporarily surrender your immediate sense of security. An unwillingness to sacrifice will hold you back. If you think you can achieve something great without sacrifice, you will stay glued to where you are, because rarely is this the case. To move forward you may have to give up safe but unrewarding work. Stay receptive and be willing to reinvent yourself to take advantage of new possibilities and shed things that are no longer working.

Keep growing, learning and working to improve yourself. Whatever gifts, skills, experience and resources you have, keep improving them. Think about how different our lives would be if we looked at every day as an exciting opportunity to learn, move one step forward and contribute.

In order to grow, we need to stretch ourselves—and it isn't always comfortable. Expect this; it is part of the process. We need to get out of our comfort zone for extraordinary things to happen. The point is to stretch to where we feel uncomfortable (this means we are charting new territory), but we don't need to stretch to the point of agony. This would paralyze us and be unproductive. If we are to continue growing, the need to stretch never ends. But if we look back later, we will discover that these times of stretching enabled us to make a change and reach new heights, and we will look back fondly at those times.

We are always growing in understanding of the lessons learned throughout our entire life. This growth feeds our soul. We thrive on it and it feels great!

THE DARKNESS BEFORE THE DAWN

Before a dream is realized, the Soul of the World tests
everything that was learned along the way.
It does this not because it is evil, but so that we can,
in addition to realizing our dreams, master the lessons
we've learned as we've moved toward that dream.
That's the point at which most people give up.
It's the point at which, as we say in the language of the desert,
one 'dies of thirst just when the palm trees have appeared
on the horizon.' Every search begins with beginner's luck,
and every search ends with the victor's being severely tested.

—Paolo Coehlo, *The Alchemist*

The road is narrow and long, and there is a wilderness to pass through before you reach your destiny. The old fears, uncertainties and doubts can encircle you, but there is always someone or something to guide you just as you need it. It could be a friend, it could be your intuition or it could be a sign.

You will stumble and fall, but what matters is that you continue to give it everything you've got. There are tests, but there are also miracles if you stay focused and committed.

Often, before a breakthrough moment "everything seems to go wrong," and deep depression can cloud your consciousness. It means that the familiar doubts and fears are rising out of the subconscious to the surface, to give you a chance to address them head-on. This is the darkness before the dawn.

Imagine a small shipwreck out at sea. It is night, and very dark, and two friends are tossed in the ocean without a life raft. Their only chance is to swim to the shore a few miles away. They swim until they are exhausted and don't feel that they can take another stroke. Because it is dark, they can't see anything ahead of them except water. They have no idea where they are or even if they are going in the right direction. So one gives up and succumbs to the water and the other digs deep into his last physical and mental reserves and somehow manages to stay afloat. Very soon the earliest morning light appears and the one remaining swimmer can now see the shore. It is just on the horizon. He mourns that his friend had lost the faith and given up too soon; they were much closer than they knew. Then, with one last burst of energy, he starts to swim again and soon makes it to shore.

This literally is a story of the darkness before the dawn and the importance of not losing faith even when things look entirely bleak. One person succumbs to the doubt and fear, and the other digs deep and finds a way to keep going. Sometimes it just takes one last ounce of perseverance before you finally get a sign of encouragement and encounter the dawn.

It is at this point that you get a chance to see how strong you are; you get to see what you are made of. When you feel as if you are about to break and you can't take even a second more, that's when you dig deep, recalibrate and find your fighting spirit once again. You refuse to go down. Instead you get mad, you get strong… and then you go for it.

If you are meant to do something significant and move on into the next new dimension of your life, the Universe tests you to see if you are up to the task. I call this "getting squeezed." Difficult circumstances seem to line up to test your resolve—and it's no fun. If you are squeezed and you lose your focus or readily compromise, your progression toward your goal is slowed, or stalled. But if you get squeezed and you stay 100% committed, the Universe knows you are ready for the job. The harder you're squeezed, the larger the test. The trick is to be able to be squeezed and still maintain your integrity, determination and focus—and feel great about yourself afterward.

Whenever you get discouraged, remind yourself that as uncomfortable as it is right now, doing something is better than doing nothing at all. You are taking a step in the right direction. Let go and trust what lays ahead for you, even if you don't know exactly what it looks like.

The spiritual path that leads you to your destiny is not an easy one. That's why a friend and I once joked that if you're really upset with a person, instead of sending them ill will, wish them spiritual growth. Ultimately it's good; it's what our souls want and need, but it's guaranteed to be painful as we come face to face with our biggest issues.

This also frees you of the burden of wasting valuable energy by trying to personally affect an outcome. Try your best and then let the Universe help you.

This is a time for us to show our resolve and commitment, to prove that we've mastered the lessons we've learned along the way. It's tempting, preferable and logical to think that the universe should cut us some slack at this point, but we can't expect the easy route. Sometimes we get it, sometimes we don't.

One thing to fall back on—although sometimes we prefer to talk ourselves out of it, we always know the right thing deep down.

It's a time to show the fabric we're made of. Upon reflection when we look back, we know the tests only made us stronger.

Own your destiny and make your soul unsellable. By knowing yourself completely (heart and soul, vision and commitments), you will have the resolve to stand firm and keep going. To do this, active faith is always essential.

13

FULFILLMENT

A musician must make music, an artist must paint,
a poet must write if he is to be ultimately at peace with himself.
What one can be, one must be.

—Abraham Maslow

Fulfillment begins the moment you acknowledge that you have a gift and you begin applying it in your own special way. You become grateful for your differences from others. You realize that you have a mission and are making a difference. You are learning, growing and accomplishing something special in your life.

Your true purpose is your highest good and it brings you great joy. If it is *your* highest good, it is the highest good of others and/or the planet as well. It is not enough to keep it to yourself. You could be creating a new drug, providing entertainment to the weary, being a foster parent to a child or lighting the imagination of students with your passion for teaching. No matter what you do, you have an impact on someone or something.

You are born to be an instructor and share your gift with others. You have gained wisdom and perspective from which others will learn and benefit. This gives you a sense of genuine contribution. You lead because you demonstrate a way that others can follow.

One of the finest moments is when you shift your mentality from "what's in it for me" to "how can I benefit others." The purpose of life is to matter, to be productive, to make a difference. It is a change in thinking to "How can I master the gifts, skills and experience I've been given and use them to help in a meaningful way?" In other words, we feel fulfillment based on what we invest, what we give, what we put in.

SEEING THE LIGHT

What we have done for ourselves alone dies with us.
What we have done for others and the world remains
and is immortal.

—Albert Pike

Plato discusses the transformation from inner focus to outer focus in his famous *Allegory of the Cave*. He talks about the unenlightened becoming enlightened and their responsibility to share this gift with others.

The *Allegory* describes prisoners who have been chained since childhood inside a cave. Behind the prisoners is a fire. There is also a walkway along which animals walk, and various plants and other things are carried. The shapes cast a shadow on the wall, and the prisoners can only see these shadows. They are chained in a way that they cannot turn around and see the fire.

Suppose a prisoner is released—he is dragged up out of the cave and into the sunlight. At first his eyes will be so blinded that he will not be able to see anything. Then he will be able to see darker shapes such as the shadows. At first, "the shadows that he formerly saw are truer than the objects which are now shown to him." This is because this was his reality for all of his life up to this point. This was his comfort zone. Eventually he will see brighter and brighter objects and finally he will be able to see the sun. At that point, he will see true reality—the world as it is—not the world of shadows that defined his existence before.

Plato describes the sun as the source of true knowledge. He says that the prisoners represent much of humanity, who have not seen the truth. However, the freed men (the enlightened) will begin to loosen the chains which are representative of our society and/or outside influences. They serve to stop us from questioning.

However, not all men want to be freed from the cave. They prefer to stay in the complacency of their restricted life.

Plato goes on to say that if a prisoner were to break out of his chains and turn around, he would be temporarily dazzled by the light. His eyes would acclimate and he would be able to find his way and exit the cave. But this is a difficult and scary process. He would be defying the guards, society as he knows it and his normal way of life. The majority of prisoners do not want to break free. It is too unsettling, too risky. Even if they have been miserable in their surroundings, the fear of the unknown is too great. They have reconciled to their existence and choose not to venture.

Paradoxically, if the man who had seen the sunlight were then to return to the darkness of the cave, his eyes would be weak from adjusting back into the darkness. And if there were a contest to compete for stature about measuring the shadows on the wall, he would be disadvantaged while his eyes acclimated again. The prisoners, the unenlightened, who had been there all along would then say in their ignorance that it was better not to even think of ascending.

Plato calls the journey upward to be the ascent of the soul.

His *Allegory of the Cave* is an allegory of life. There are several key lessons that parallel our modern existence.

> We can easily get wrapped up in our existence, the outside world, our persona. We can convince ourselves that a life of seeing shadows is okay—however limiting it may be.
>
> Even if given a chance, very few decide to venture.
>
> Most of those who do not venture will not understand those who do.
>
> Those who do venture and "see the light" have trouble going back into the darkness. Yet these very people are the ones best suited to lead.

In the *Allegory of the Cave*, Plato symbolically describes the predicament that mankind finds itself in and suggests that to resolve this predicament, enlightened individuals have an obligation to the rest of society.

When you are free, you can help liberate others.

They who, in Plato's words, "are truly rich, not in silver and gold, but in virtue and wisdom" have an obligation to share their blessings—"to lead and serve others."

The prisoners are like us until we reclaim our full abilities and remember our power. Most refused to believe in the glory of the light that awaited them outside; they refused to venture out and see. Yet there were a few who might welcome the chance to learn if they were freed and guided. Just imagine how much they would benefit if they had an "enlightened," experienced person available to guide them.

Great leaps forward are born in a few people at first and then the ideas spread to others. You are a front runner for bringing this awareness and making these changes. You can help make the world a better place. Whatever gift you have, it is your calling to share it. If you keep it bottled up, it will make you uneasy. You'll feel unsettled. If you share it, you'll feel rewarded.

It's like all along you've had a sense that something is missing—that you've had a hole in your heart. When you share and give back to others, you begin to fill that hole. And you feel "whole." It's a great feeling and brings tremendous satisfaction. In reality, what seems on the outside to be a one-way street of helping others, is actually a two-way street of helping you as well. Giving is a gift to the giver.

As the examples in this book—Mark Misage, Trevor Romain and Caroline Boudreaux—have demonstrated, you don't need to be famous to make a difference. You can be an ordinary person who does extraordinary things. One human being can affect many other people and touch their lives in a very special way. We do not need to save the world, but simply make a difference to someone or something. You can't always measure your own impact right away. It may be that you make an invention that improves people's lives a decade before its time, but others reap the benefit in the future.

We know that what we are meant to do is something greater than ourselves. Once we tap into it, we feel an urgency, an insatiable desire to continually make progress. We feel that we are on a mission and our quest is never done. The truth is, we don't want it to be done because it brings us great joy. It consumes us. It excites us. No matter how much we accomplish, there will always be more. Yet it hardly feels like work—it is a labor of love. You can barely distinguish between work and play. Sure you have to make some sacrifices, but when you evaluate it over time, you know it was worth it. The sacrifices you made enabled some of your finest accomplishments. In the end, it all matters. We can feel the meaning and we feel that we are genuinely living instead of running in the rat race. It's invigorating and we're compelled to keep going until we have reached our full potential. It's a life-long endeavor.

Fulfillment is given to those who use the gifts the Universe bestowed upon them to the fullest. When we express our full potential, we find that special joy that comes from within us. We are motivated to make a contribution.

To whom much is given, much is expected. With the gifts that we were given comes a responsibility. They were given to us for a worthy and much needed purpose, and we are responsible for fully using them. We are called to live extraordinary lives and bring our gifts to the world. The beauty is that when we genuinely give, we also receive. When we help others we receive a blessing—a great sense of satisfaction—that little by little fills the hole in our heart. We regain our creativity and our enthusiasm, and the empty feeling we had walked around with for so long disappears. We know that we are doing what we can, moment by moment, to make the world a better place.

Here is what you can expect when you follow your Professional Destiny:

You are expressing yourself. You are using all of the talent and energy within, and you feel like you are realizing your full creative potential.

Your happiness is transparent. Your passion shows in your eyes and in your smile. You're aware of what your life is about and look forward to beginning each day. You have a deep inner satisfaction that gives you an air of confidence. Work doesn't feel like work—you're doing it because it is what you want to do.

You are not motivated by money alone. You are motivated first and foremost by a sense of genuine contribution. Your purpose in living is to find the perfection of your gift, being the best at it and sharing it with others. This gives you a tireless source of energy and motivates you above all.

Your potential is magnified. You feel empowered—there is little you can't do and you become better at accomplishing things. You take more ownership, which increases the quality of all that you touch.

You are fulfilled. There is nothing more fulfilling than reaching out and touching perfection in the thing that you most love to do.

Your dreams stay big. You fully give the energy of your mind and the enthusiasm of your heart, and you will do something that matters—boldly and deliberately. You come into the flow of your life, and this is one of life's greatest gifts.

You feel an inner peace. Your spiritual beliefs and ability to make a living are in harmony. You feel wiser— as if you are becoming the person you always knew you were.

You are complete. You are practicing your gifts with full conviction and experience the difference you are making in the world. Instead of feeling a hole in your existence, you feel whole and vital. You have much to give and joyously express your potential. Because of this, you leave a magnificent legacy behind.

Our single most important responsibility in life is to figure out who we are in the grandest sense and what we came here to do. We must fully express our gifts. It is our life's work. When we discover this and live it, we have a sense of deep satisfaction. We feel familiar, like we are coming home.

We have found our Professional Destiny.

What they're saying about *Professional Destiny*

"Valerie Hausladen inspires readers to bridge the gap between the professional and personal by reminding us that passion should be our driving force in life, whether at home or in the workplace."
— Bob Gutermuth, President, The Dialog Group

"Five stars for this incredible book. It is one that everyone should read at least once. Valerie's writing comes from a place deep in her heart. It's an inspirational 'how to' book on how to find the work you will enjoy for the rest of your life."
— Caroline Boudreaux, Founder, The Miracle Foundation

"If you're looking for an accessible read of some profound ideas about leading a worthwhile professional life, this book is for you. It brings spiritual ideas into the arena of the practical, showing how we can all get more from and give more to the world of work."
— Fred Vetter, Organizational and Management Consultant

"If you are interested in a job that is bigger than money, a job that is about destiny and a life of accomplishment, here's your manual. Read it as if your life and career depended on it."
— Perch Ducote, Author, *The Soul Of Communications*

"Valerie Hausladen creates value from principles. She is a gift to all of us blessed to work with her and to benefit from her grace and wisdom."
— Casey Jones, Senior VP, Dell Inc.